T0089039

"John Piper remains a trustworthy and faithful voice, urging God's people to behold, partake of, delight in, and live for the glory of God. With rare purity and passion, Piper's writing causes the reader to think less about the author and more about the object of his affection, his glorious and sovereign Lord."

STEVE GREEN

"John Piper has helped me to see the Lord. He has been a broken vessel who has pushed me to pursue deeper pleasures. And I now live life and read Scripture through the filter of delighting myself in the Lord—for His glory—and for my joy."

SHANE BARNARD

"God has blessed my whole family through the writings of John Piper. From his books, we have learned about a sovereign God whose goal is His own glory and the joy of His people. Piper continues to help us recover a biblical view of God."

ED NALLE, GLAD

"I am honored to know John as a pastor and a friend. He has been both to me since the founding of the Passion movement. So much of his godly wisdom and teaching have been a lighted path for me in the increasingly hazy days we live in."

CHRIS TOMLIN

"Very few people have inspired us in quite the same way that Piper has. His shameless preaching of the truth always kicks us in the teeth, challenging us to evaluate our lives, our worldview, and our understanding of God."

CAEDMON'S CALL

"Not only has my spiritual walk been encouraged by *Desiring God*, but also by so many of John Piper's writings and sermons. I will forever live my life trying to remember the important message I have learned from Pastor Piper to 'glorify God by enjoying Him forever.'"

MAC POWELL, THIRD DAY

"John Piper's writings consistently draw me to cherish all God is for us in Christ. His insistence that God intends us to passionately pursue joy in Him alone has influenced not only the way I lead worship and write songs, but the way I live my life. When I first met John I told him, 'Your books have caused me to love the Savior more.' For that reason, I thank God for John Piper."

BOB KAUFLIN, DIRECTOR OF WORSHIP
DEVELOPMENT, SOVEREIGN GRACE MINISTRIES

"John Piper's books continue to renew my sense of wonder at the mystery and wildness of our Creator God. I am thankful for his sensitivity to both the head and the heart of the gospel of Jesus."

CHARLIE LOWELL, JARS OF CLAY

LIFE
as a
VAPOR

JOHN
PIPER

MULTNOMAH

LIFE AS A VAPOR

© 2004 by Desiring God Foundation

International Standard Book Number: 978-0-525-65340-0

Cover design by PixelWorks Studio

Unless otherwise indicated, Scripture quotations are from:
The Holy Bible, English Standard Version
© 2001 by Crossway Bibles, a division of Good News Publishers.
Used by permission. All rights reserved.

Other Scripture quotations are from:
New American Standard Bible (NASB)
© 1960, 1977 by the Lockman Foundation
Revised Standard Version Bible (RSV)
© 1946, 1952 by the Division of Christian Education
of the National Council of the Churches of Christ
in the United States of America
The Holy Bible, New King James Version (NKJV)
© 1984 by Thomas Nelson, Inc.
Italics in Scripture quotations indicate emphasis added.

Published in the United States by Multnomah, an imprint of the Crown
Publishing Group, a division of Penguin Random House LLC, New York.

MULTNOMAH® and its mountain colophon are registered trademarks
of Penguin Random House LLC.

147028622

BOOKS BY JOHN PIPER

The Pleasures of God

Desiring God

The Dangerous Duty of Delight

Future Grace

A Hunger for God

Let the Nations Be Glad!

Seeing and Savoring Jesus Christ

The Legacy of Sovereign Joy

The Hidden Smile of God

The Roots of Endurance

The Misery of Job and the Mercy of God
(with photography by Ric Ergenbright)

The Innkeeper

Recovering Biblical Manhood and Womanhood
(edited with Wayne Grudem)

What's the Difference?

The Justification of God

Counted Righteous in Christ

Brothers, We Are Not Professionals

The Supremacy of God in Preaching

Beyond the Bounds
(edited with Justin Taylor and Paul Kjoss Helseth)

God's Passion for His Glory

A God-Entranced Vision of All Things
(edited with Justin Taylor)

Don't Waste Your Life

The Prodigal's Sister

A Godward Life

A Godward Life, Book Two

Pierced by the Word

To the children
whose funerals I have done
with gratitude for the painful lesson that,
short or long, life is a vapor

You do not know what your life will be like tomorrow.
You are just a vapor that appears for a little while
and then vanishes away.

JAMES 4:14, NASB

TABLE OF CONTENTS

A WORD TO THE READER

The Son of God is not a vapor. He is solid reality, with no beginning and no ending. His name is Jesus Christ. He is the same yesterday and today and forever. He looked His disciples in the eye and said without irony or exaggeration, "Before Abraham was, I am."

But what about us? Once we were not, and now we exist? With the conception of all five of our children, that stunned me. Suddenly my wife is pregnant. A human has come into being. For how long? Forever. Either in heaven or in hell. There is no going out of existence. For that would not be joy for those who love God nor punishment for those who don't.

You exist forever. There is no use protesting that you did not ask to exist and would like not to. That is not an option. You and God are both in the universe to stay—either as friends on His terms, or enemies.

Which it will be is proven in this life. And this life is a vapor. Two seconds, and we will be gone—to heaven or to hell. "As for man, his days are like grass; he flourishes like a flower of the field; for the wind passes over it, and it is gone" (Psalm 103:15–16).

Jesus Christ came into this world—this fleeting, fallen, fickle world—and did the greatest thing that will ever be done. As the perfect Son of God, He died in our place, absorbed the wrath of God, paid the penalty for sin, provided the righteousness of the law, and rose invincible from the dead—all in a vapor's life of thirty-three years.

Because of that, we have something firm to grasp. "Surely the people are grass. The grass withers, the flower fades, but the word of our God will stand forever" (Isaiah 40:7–8). The gospel is firm and lasts forever. My prayer is that these meditations on the Word of God will link you with eternal joy, and make the vapor of your life an everlasting aroma of praise to the glory of Christ.

John Piper

One

DOES IT MATTER
WHAT OTHERS THINK?

Life is too short to spend time and energy worrying about what others think of us. Or should we care about what others think precisely because that really matters in this short life? Should we be radically free from what others think, so that we don't fall into the indictment of being a "second-hander" or "man-pleaser," a slave to expediency? Or should we keep an eye out for what others think of what we do, so that we don't fall into the indictment of being boorish and insensitive and offensive? The answer is not simple. Some biblical texts seem to say it matters what others think. Others seem to say it doesn't.

For example, Jesus warned us: "Woe to you, when all people speak well of you" (Luke 6:26). And His own enemies saw in Him an indifference to what others thought:

"Teacher, we know that you are true and do not care about anyone's opinion. For you are not swayed by appearances, but truly teach the way of God" (Mark 12:14). Paul said that if he tried to please men he would no longer be serving Christ: "Am I now seeking the approval of man, or of God? Or am I trying to please man? If I were still trying to please man, I would not be a servant of Christ" (Galatians 1:10). "As we have been approved by God to be entrusted with the gospel, so we speak, not to please man, but to please God who tests our hearts" (1 Thessalonians 2:4). So it seems that Christians should not care much about what others think.

On the other hand, Proverbs 22:1 says, "A good name is to be chosen rather than great riches, and favor is better than silver or gold." This sounds like reputation matters. And Paul was vigilant that he not be discredited in his handling the money he collected for the poor: "[We are] taking precaution so that no one will discredit us in our administration of this generous gift; for we have regard for what is honorable, not only in the sight of the Lord, but also in the sight of men" (2 Corinthians 8:20–21, NASB). It mattered what men thought.

Paul taught the Roman church, "Now we who are strong ought...not just please ourselves. Each of us is to please his neighbor for his good, to his edification" (Romans 15:1–2, NASB). And he taught that one of the qualifications for elders is that they must be "above reproach" (1 Timothy

3:2), including among unbelievers: "He must be well thought of by outsiders, so that he may not fall into disgrace, into a snare of the devil" (1 Timothy 3:7).

Similarly Peter charged us to care about what outsiders thought: "Keep your behavior excellent among the Gentiles, so that in the thing in which they slander you as evildoers, they may because of your good deeds, as they observe them, glorify God in the day of visitation" (1 Peter 2:12, NASB).

Question: How is the tension between these two groups of passages to be resolved?

Answer: By realizing that our aim in life is that "Christ will be magnified in my body, whether by life or by death" (Philippians 1:20, NKJV). In other words, with Paul, we do care—really care—about what others think *of Christ*. Their salvation hangs on what they think of Christ. And our lives are to display His truth and beauty. So we *must* care what others think of us *as representative of Christ*. Love demands it.

But we ought not to care much what others think of us for our own sake. Our concern is ultimately for Christ's reputation, not ours. The accent falls not on our value or excellence or virtue or power or wisdom. It falls on whether *Christ* is honored by the way people think of us. Does Christ get a good reputation because of the way we live? Is the excellence of Christ displayed in our lives? That should matter to us, not whether we ourselves are praised.

Again notice a crucial distinction: The litmus test of our faithfully displaying the truth and beauty of Christ in our lives is *not* in the opinion of others. We want them to see Christ in us and love Him (and thus, very incidentally, to approve of us). When John the Baptist said, "He must increase, but I must decrease" (John 3:30), he spoke for every true Christian. We must insist on being less than Christ. I am vigilant, as far as it depends on me, to be less than Christ to others.

But we know others may be blind to spiritual reality and resistant to Christ. So they may think more of us than they thought of Him. Or they may think less of us than they think of Him, *not* because they think well of Him, but, as Jesus said, "If they have called the master of the house Beelzebul, how much more will they malign those of his household" (Matthew 10:25). They may think He is a devil and we are worse. Jesus wanted men to admire Him and trust Him. That would have been their salvation. But He did not change who He was in order to win their approval. Nor can we change who He was, or who we are in Him.

Yes, we want people to look on us with approval when we are displaying that Jesus is infinitely valuable to us. But we dare not make the opinion of others the measure of our faithfulness. They may be blind and resistant to truth. Then the reproach we bear is no sign of our unfaithfulness or lack of love.

Father, at times the way of Christ is complex
to our sin-stained and finite minds.
Forgive us for the times we have justified
our vanity in the name of a good reputation.
O, Lord, grant us, in this brief life,
the wisdom and courage
to please others, or not to please others,
for the sake of Christ alone,
and not our own praise.
In Jesus' name,
Amen.

Two

SUFFERING, MERCY, AND HEAVENLY REGRET

When I think of the atrocities in the world, like the genocides of the twentieth century, it makes me want to live my short life on earth with as few regrets as possible. Germans killing Jews during World War II (6 million); Turks killing Armenians, 1914–1915 (1.5 million); Stalin killing 60 million people in Russia during his Communist regime in the 1930's and 1940's; the Khmer Rouge killing Cambodians, 1975–1979 (2 million); Saddam Hussein's troops killing Iraqi Kurds, 1987–1988 (100,000); Serbs killing Bosnian Muslims, 1992–1995 (200,000); Hutus killing Tutsis, 1994 (800,000); Americans killing unborn children, 1973–present (40 million). There were others.

Add to this the suffering owing to natural disasters like the tropical storm in November 1970 that killed about

400,000 people in Bangladesh, or the earthquake of Gujarat, India, in January 2001 that killed 15,000, or the AIDS epidemic in Africa that has taken the lives of 2.5 million people. Then add the sadness and pain and eventual death of your own family. When I think on these things, it makes me tremble at the prospect of living a trivial, self-serving, comfortable, middle-class, ordinary, untroubled American life. I can't keep eternity out of my mind. Life is short and eternity is long. Very long. It is a long time to regret a wasted life.

Which raises the question: Is there regret in heaven? Can regret be part of the ever-increasing, unspeakable joy of the age to come, purchased by Jesus Christ (Romans 8:32)? My answer is yes. I am aware of promises like Revelation 21:4, "He will wipe away every tear from their eyes, and death shall be no more, neither shall there be mourning nor crying nor pain anymore, for the former things have passed away." But I don't think this rules out tears of joy, and it may not rule out regretful joy.

Why do I think this? I do not see how we will be able to worship Christ and sing the song of the Lamb without a clear memory of the glorious, saving work of Jesus Christ and all that it involved. According to Revelation 5:9, the saints will sing "a new song, saying, 'Worthy are you to take the scroll and to open its seals, for you were slain, and by your blood you ransomed people for God from every tribe and language and people and nation.'" But ransomed from what? Will we have forgotten? This song and this memory will make no sense without the memory of sin. And the memory of sin will be hypocritical without the confession that it was our sin that Jesus died for.

It is inconceivable to me that we will remember our sin for what it really was, and the suffering of Christ for what it really was, and not feel regretful joy. The intensity of our joy in grace will be fed by the remembrance of our unworthiness. "He who is forgiven little, loves little" (Luke 7:47). But this does *not* mean we should sin so "that grace may abound" (Romans 6:1). The holiest will be the happiest. But it does mean that regret will not ruin heaven. There will be kinds of joys, and complexities of happiness, and combinations of emotions in heaven of which we have never dreamed.

But all this leaves me trembling that I not throw away the one short life that I will look back on for all eternity. Just think of it. You have one life. One very short life. Then an eternity to remember. Does not the suffering in this world seem inexplicable to you? Is not this great, global (and intensely personal) suffering a call to magnify the mercy of Christ by how we respond? Is not suffering a seamless fabric, stretching into eternity for unbelievers? And therefore, are not Christians the only people who can respond with helpful relief to the *totality* of misery? Unbelievers may relieve some suffering in this vapor's breath of life on earth. But beyond that they are no help at all.

Shall we not then live our lives—and prepare for heaven—by strategizing in all our vocations, and with all our talents and all our money, to relieve suffering (now and forever) for the glory of Jesus? The twentieth century was the bloodiest and cruelest of all centuries. Man is not getting better. But God will hold us accountable in the age to come not for what others have done. He will call us to account for what blood-bought hope freed us to do for others in the name of Christ. We will give joyful and tearful thanks in that day for the grace that covered our sin and the grace that caused our love.

Father in heaven, have mercy on
the misery of this world.
Forgive us for our part in
causing the pain of others.
Waken us as never before to the preciousness
of your mercy bought by the blood of Christ.
Fix our hopes so fully on the joy of heaven,
that we become the freest of all people on earth.
May our everlasting memories of your grace
make us glad of all you changed
and all you forgave.
In Jesus' name,
Amen.

Three

THE EYE IS THE LAMP OF THE BODY

A Meditation on Matthew 6:19–24

Do not lay up for yourselves treasures on earth, where moth and rust destroy and where thieves break in and steal, 20 but lay up for yourselves treasures in heaven, where neither moth nor rust destroys and where thieves do not break in and steal. 21 For where your treasure is, there your heart will be also. 22 The eye is the lamp of the body. So, if your eye is healthy, your whole body will be full of light, 23 but if your eye is bad, your whole body will be full of darkness. If then the light in you is darkness, how great is the darkness! 24 No one can serve two masters, for either he will hate the one and love the other, or he will be devoted to the one and despise the other. You cannot serve God and money.

Sandwiched between the command to lay up treasures in heaven (6:19–21) and the warning that you can't serve God and money (6:24) are the strange words about the eye being the lamp of the body. If the eye is good, or healthy (literally, "if the eye is single"), the whole body will be full of light. But if the eye is bad, the body will be full of darkness. In other words: How you see reality determines whether you are in the dark or not.

Now why is this saying about the good and bad eye sandwiched between two teachings on money? I think it's because the specific thing about seeing that shows the eye is good is how it sees God in relation to money and all it can buy. That's the issue on either side of the sandwich meat of Matthew 6:22–23. In Matthew 6:19–21 the issue is: You should desire heaven-reward not earth-reward. Which, in short, means: desire God not money. In Matthew 6:24 the issue is whether you can serve two masters. Answer: You cannot serve God and money.

This is a double description of light! If you are laying up treasures in heaven not earth, you are walking in the light. If you are serving God not money, you are walking in the light.

Between these two descriptions of the light, Jesus says that the eye is the lamp of the body and that a good eye produces a fullness of this light. So what is the good eye that gives so much light and the bad eye that leaves us in the dark?

One clue is found in Matthew 20:15. Jesus has just said, in a parable, that men who worked one hour will be paid the same as those who worked all day, because the master is merciful, and besides, they all agreed to their wage. Those who worked all day grumbled that the men who worked one hour were paid too much. Jesus responded with the surprising words found here in Matthew 6:23, "Is your eye bad because I am good?" (ESV margin, a good, but perplexing, literal translation).

What is bad about their eye? What's bad is that their eye does not see the mercy of the master as beautiful. He gives generously to those who worked only an hour. The all-day workers see it as ugly. They don't see reality for what it is. They do not have an eye that can see mercy as more precious than money.

Now bring that understanding of the bad eye back to Matthew 6:23 and let it determine the meaning of the healthy eye.

> The eye is the lamp of the body. So, if your eye is healthy, your whole body will be full of light, 23but if your eye is bad, your whole body will be full of darkness. If then the light in you is darkness, how great is the darkness!

What would the healthy eye be that fills us with light? It would be an eye that sees the Master's generosity as more precious than money. The healthy eye sees God and His ways as the great Treasure in life, not money.

You have a healthy eye if you look on heaven and love to maximize the reward of God's fellowship there. You have a healthy eye if you look at Master-money and Master-God and see Master-God as infinitely more valuable and desirable. In other words, a healthy eye is a valuing eye, a discerning eye, a treasuring eye. It doesn't just see facts about money and God. It doesn't just perceive what is true and false. It sees and assesses the true difference between beauty and ugliness, it senses value and worthlessness, it discerns what is really desirable and what is undesirable. The seeing of the healthy eye is not neutral. When it sees God, it sees God-as-beautiful. It sees God-as-desirable.

That is why the healthy eye leads to the path of light: laying up treasures in heaven and serving God not money. The healthy eye is a single eye. It has one Treasure. God. When that happens in your life, you are full of light.

*Gracious Father of light,
give us eyes to see Your worth.
Heal our blindness. Save us from the
deadly disease of seeing the world
as worth more than its Maker.
Restore the capacity of our hearts to cherish
infinite beauty and savor infinite sweetness.
Deliver us from the deadening effects
of thinking this short life is the main thing.
In Jesus' name, we pray,
Amen.*

Four

MY LIFE IS A VAPOR

A Meditation on James 4:13–16

Come now, you who say, "Today or tomorrow we will go into such and such a town and spend a year there and trade and make a profit"— [14] yet you do not know what tomorrow will bring. What is your life? For you are a mist that appears for a little time and then vanishes. [15] Instead you ought to say, "If the Lord wills, we will live and do this or that." [16]As it is, you boast in your arrogance. All such boasting is evil.

When it comes to how we think and talk about our business plans, our mind-set and our mouth matter. According to Jesus' brother James, the person who says, "Tomorrow we will go to Denver and do business," is arrogant. He does not comprehend in his pride that his life is like a vapor and that God, not he, will decide if he lives and goes to Denver (or gets out of bed) tomorrow.

I can imagine some American pragmatist saying, "What practical difference would it make in my business planning whether I believe my life is a vapor? Do I stop planning because my life may be short or uncertain?" I think James would say, "No, you don't stop planning. You don't drop out of society. You don't become a hermit, waiting for your little vapor of life to disappear."

So what is the point? The point is that for James, and for God, it matters whether a true view of life informs and shapes the way you *think*, and how you speak about your plans. Your mind-set matters. How you *talk* about your plans matters.

Ponder this. Believing that your life is a vapor may make no practical, bottom-line difference in whether you plan to do business in a place for one month or one year or ten years. But, in James's mind—and he speaks for God—it makes a difference how you think about it and talk about it. "Come now you who *say*...." Saying the wrong thing about your plans matters.

Why? Why does that matter? Because God created us not just to do things and go places with our bodies, but to have certain attitudes and convictions and verbal descriptions that reflect a true view of life and God. God means for the truth about Himself and about life to be known and felt and spoken as part of our reason for being. You weren't just created to go to Denver and do business; you were created to go to Denver with thoughts and attitudes and words that reflect a right view of God.

So James says in verse 14, in all your planning, keep in your mind, and express with your lips, this truth: "You are a vapor that appears for a little while and then vanishes away." That is, keep in mind that you have no firm substance on this earth. You are as fragile as a mist. Keep in mind that you have no durability on this earth, for you appear "for a little while"—just a little while. Your time is short. And keep in mind that you will disappear. You will be gone, and life will go on without you. It matters, he says, that you keep this view of life in mind.

Then verse 15 tells us the true view of God that we should have in our minds, and in our mouths, as we imagine our future—as we plot our investments and make our plans. Verse 13 began, "Come now, you who say, 'Today or tomorrow we will go into such and such a town and spend a year there and make a profit.'" Now he tells us what's wrong with that way of talking. He says in verse 15, "Instead, you ought to say, '*If the Lord wills*, we will live and also do this or that.'"

In other words, it not only matters that you have a right view of life when you make your plans (because you are like a vapor), but it also matters that you have a right view of God as you make your plans. And it matters that you give expression of this true view of God: "You ought to say—say!—, 'If the Lord wills, we will live and also do this or that.'"

So what is the right view of God that he teaches us to have in verse 15? He tells us two very important things about God. One is contained in the words: "If the Lord wills, we will live." And the other is contained in the words, "If the Lord wills, we will...do this or that." How would you state the truth about God contained in each of those two sentences?

I will leave it for you to answer. But don't miss the obvious: Scripture puts a premium on how we think and how we talk. This is not surprising. Above all the animals humans are created in the image of God with thought and language beyond all comparison. This gift is not gratuitous. It is meant to make the glory of God known. If He wills we live. If He wills we act. We have minds and tongues to speak this truly for all the world to hear.

Omnipotent, all-governing Father,
not a bird falls to the ground apart from You,
and not a hair of our heads turns gray apart from You.
Grant that we may know these great truths about You,
and that we may speak them with winsome joy.
Forgive us for the arrogance of denying them,
and for the pride of vaunted self-sufficiency.
Make us like children
in our daily reliance
on You, we pray.
In Jesus' name,
Amen.

Five

GOD'S FAVORITE COLOR

Pondering Why Worry Doesn't Work

I remember walking to Oudall's Used Book Store with my colleague Tom Steller. We were discussing Jesus' words about anxiety. As I quoted the sentence, "Which of you by being anxious can add a single cubit to his span of life?" I stepped onto Portland Avenue and almost got run over.

Which, of course, set me to thinking: *Well, I suppose you really can add a cubit to your span of life if you are anxious enough to watch the light.* Now, of course, street-crossing was not so dangerous in Jesus' day. But surely He would have agreed that you *can* add a cubit to your span of life if you don't walk into the desert so far that you die of thirst trying to walk out again. And if desert-phobia keeps you from doing that, then does not anxiety add to your span of life?

No! It is not the anxiety which saves. It is reasonable

precaution. The desire not to die in the desert is not the same as anxiety about walking in the desert. Anxiety is the twisty, tense, fearful feeling inside that may or may not go with reasonable precaution; and it is the caution that can add a cubit to your life, not bad feelings. Precautions have lengthened many lives; anxiety has lengthened none and shortened many.

"Do not be anxious about your life" (Luke 12:22) does not mean: Walk on red (at least not always). It means don't fantasize nervously about getting pasted in the crosswalk. It means believe that, if you do get pasted, God is still in control and you will be with Him and He will take care of your family. It means that if a carton of gold is across the street and the kingdom of God is on this side, don't cross even on green. It means that if a red light tries to stop you from giving generously and sacrificially to the poor and to missions this week, walk on red! Financial precautions are almost always too conservative. After blue, God's favorite color is green. Consider how the lilies grow.

Father, deliver us from the self-deception
that makes us believe anxiety is mere precaution,
and that unfaithful precaution is
anything other than cloaked anxiety.
O, how devious is the self-protecting soul!
Have mercy on us, and make us bold.
Free us from fear and from
prudential avoidances of love.
Make us more eager for the joy of giving
than for the security of keeping.
In Jesus' name,
Amen.

Six

KILL ANGER
BEFORE IT KILLS YOU
OR YOUR MARRIAGE

In marriage, anger rivals lust as a killer. My guess is that anger is a worse enemy than lust. It also destroys other kinds of camaraderie. Some people have more anger than they think, because it has disguises. When willpower hinders rage, anger smolders beneath the surface, and the teeth of the soul grind with frustration.

It can come out in tears that look more like hurt. But the heart has learned that this may be the only way to hurt back. It may come out as silence because we have resolved not to fight. It may show up in picky criticism and relentless correction. It may strike out at persons that have nothing to do with its origin. It will often feel warranted by how wrongly it has been treated. After all, Jesus got angry (Mark 3:5), and Paul says, "Be angry and do not sin" (Ephesians 4:26).

However, good anger among fallen people is rare. That's why James says, "Be quick to hear, slow to speak, slow to anger; for the anger of man does not produce the righteousness that God requires" (James 1:19–20). And Paul says, "Men should pray, lifting holy hands without anger or quarreling" (1 Timothy 2:8). "Let all bitterness and wrath and anger and clamor and slander be put away from you" (Ephesians 4:31).

Therefore, one of the greatest battles of life is the battle to "put away anger," not just control its expressions. I invite you to join me in this battle by adding these nine biblical weapons to your arsenal.

1. *Ponder the right of Christ to be angry, but how He endured the cross, as an example of long-suffering.* "For to this you have been called, because Christ also suffered for you, leaving you an example, so that you might follow in his steps" (1 Peter 2:21).

2. *Ponder how much you have been forgiven, and how much mercy you have been shown.* "Be kind to one another, tenderhearted, forgiving one another, as God in Christ forgave you" (Ephesians 4:32).

3. *Ponder your own sinfulness and take the beam out of your own eye.* "Why do you see the speck that is in

your brother's eye, but do not notice the log that is in your own eye? Or how can you say to your brother, 'Let me take the speck out of your eye,' when there is the log in your own eye? You hypocrite, first take the log out of your own eye, and then you will see clearly to take the speck out of your brother's eye" (Matthew 7:3–5).

4. *Ponder how harbored anger gives place to the devil.* You do not want to make room for him or invite him into your life. "Be angry and do not sin; do not let the sun go down on your anger, and give no opportunity to the devil" (Ephesians 4:26–27).

5. *Ponder the folly of your own self-immolation, that is, the numerous detrimental effects of anger to the one who is angry—some spiritual, some mental, some physical, and some relational.* "Be not wise in your own eyes; fear the LORD, and turn away from evil. It will be healing to your flesh and refreshment to your bones" (Proverbs 3:7–8).

6. *Confess your sin of anger to some trusted friend, and, if possible, to the offender.* This is a great healing act. "Therefore, confess your sins to one another and pray for one another, that you may be healed" (James 5:16).

7. *Let your anger be the key to unlock the dungeons of pride and self-pity in your heart and replace them with love.* "Love is patient and kind; love does not envy or boast; it is not arrogant or rude. It does not insist on

its own way; it is not irritable or resentful; it does not rejoice at wrongdoing, but rejoices with the truth. Love bears all things, believes all things, hopes all things, endures all things" (1 Corinthians 13:4–7).

8. *Remember that God is going to work all your frustrating circumstances for your good as you trust in His future grace.* Your offender is even doing you good, if you will respond with love. "And we know that for those who love God all things work together for good, for those who are called according to his purpose" (Romans 8:28). "Count it all joy, my brothers, when you meet trials of various kinds, for you know that the testing of your faith produces steadfastness. And let steadfastness have its full effect, that you may be perfect and complete, lacking in nothing" (James 1:2–4).

9. *Remember that God will vindicate your just cause and settle all accounts better than you could.* Either your offender will pay in hell, or Christ has paid for him. Your payback would be either double jeopardy or an offense to the cross. "Beloved, never avenge yourselves, but leave it to the wrath of God, for it is written, 'Vengeance is mine, I will repay, says the Lord'" (Romans 12:19). "When he was reviled, he did not revile in return; when he suffered, he did not threaten, but continued entrusting [his cause] to him who judges justly" (1 Peter 2:23).

Father, I love Your patience toward me.
I love it when You describe Yourself as slow
to anger and abounding in steadfast love.
Oh, to be more like You!
Have mercy on my easily angered heart!
Forgive my many peeves and murmuring.
Grant that I would be saturated with grace,
and let me show it to others as
I desperately need it for myself.
Because of Jesus,
Amen.

Seven

"LORD, COMMAND WHAT YOU WILL, AND GIVE WHAT YOU COMMAND"

Augustine's prayer, "Lord, command what you will, and give what you command" (*Confessions*, X, 31), deeply offended Pelagius, his adversary. It implied that God not only told man what he must do, believe, and obey, but also that God gave the ability to do what He said we must do. This seemed to Pelagius to undermine human responsibility and lead straight to God's deciding ahead of time who would believe and who would not.

Second Chronicles 30:1–12 is a remarkable example of the kind of Scripture that formed Augustine's vision of

God's way of working. Hezekiah has become king in the place of several very bad kings. He "did what was right in the eyes of the LORD" (2 Chronicles 29:2). One of the ways he does right is by reinstituting the Passover which had not been heeded for a long time. So in chapter 30 he sends word to "all Israel and Judah," including Ephraim and Manasseh, that they should come to the house of the Lord to keep the Passover (30:1).

In the letters that Hezekiah sends to the tribes, the blessing of God is made strictly conditional upon the response of the people. Here is what the letters say (2 Chronicles 30:6–9):

> "O sons of Israel, return to the LORD God of Abraham, Isaac and Israel, *that* He may return to those of you who escaped and are left from the hand of the kings of Assyria. 7 Do not be like your fathers and your brothers, who were unfaithful to the LORD God of their fathers, *so that* He made them a horror, as you see. 8 Now do not stiffen your neck like your fathers, but yield to the LORD and enter His sanctuary which He has consecrated forever, and serve the LORD your God, *that* His burning anger may turn away from you.9 For *if* you return to the LORD, your brothers and your sons will find compassion before those who led them captive and will return to this land. For the

LORD your God is gracious and compassionate, and will not turn His face away from you *if* you return to Him." (NASB)

Notice carefully how the italicized words in that passage make God's blessing contingent on the human response: *"If* you return to the LORD.... *If* you return." Many people read this kind of demand from the Lord and conclude that clearly God makes His blessing contingent on our ultimately self-determining response. Some will admit that God may give some assistance to encourage us to obey Him—some measure of "prevenient grace" (grace that precedes our obedience), but they say, "These conditions in verse 9 (*"If* you return to the LORD.... *If* you return to Him....") cannot be real if God Himself decisively causes the conditions to be fulfilled (some, like the open theists, would say the conditions are not real if God even *knows* what we will do ahead of time.)

This sounds reasonable to most people: When God says: *"If* you do this, *then* I will bless you," it seems reasonable that He is waiting to see what we will do by our own self-determining power, so that He can then make His move based not on what He does, but on what we do apart from His decisive control. But the problem with this apparent "reasonable" conclusion is that it contradicts the following verses.

When Hezekiah's letter arrives among the people of Israel and Judah, here is what happens (according to 2 Chronicles 30:10–12):

> So the couriers passed from city to city through the country of Ephraim and Manasseh, and as far as Zebulun, but they laughed them to scorn and mocked them. [11] Nevertheless some men of Asher, Manasseh and Zebulun humbled themselves and came to Jerusalem. [12] The hand of God was also on Judah to give them one heart to do what the king and the princes commanded by the word of the LORD. (NASB)

Verse 12 is stunning to the "reasonable" mind that concluded from verses 6–9 that the conditions given by God implied He would wait and see if people would meet them by their self-determining power. Verse 12 says that the hand of God was on Judah to give them a heart to do what king Hezekiah was commanding from the Lord. And the word "also" in the phrase "The hand of God was *also* on Judah," implies that the humble obedience of Asher, Manasseh, and Zebulun (not just Judah) was "also" caused by the hand of the Lord.

What is remarkable here is that the biblical writer does not feel any inconsistency or contradiction in saying that the obedience of the people is a condition they must meet *and* saying that this obedience is a work of God that He produced in their hearts.

This is the sort of thing that Augustine saw in many places in the Bible, which is why he prayed, "Lord, command what you will, and give what you command."

This implies that you simply cannot take all the conditions of the Bible and pile them up and use them as an argument that man has final self-determining power to give the final and ultimate veto to God's sovereign will. We must assert the conditions as strongly as the Bible does. (*If* you return to the Lord, *then* He will save you.) But we must also *not* follow the seemingly "reasonable" inference that therefore man has ultimate self-determination to meet the conditions. The Bible teaches two things: Many of the blessings of God are conditional upon our response of faith, *and* God Himself ultimately enables that response of faith and obedience.

Therefore, we pray to God for the enablement of what He calls us to do and what He calls others to do. In fact this is exactly why prayer is necessary. Only God can do what needs to be done. We are so sinful and so rebellious and so hard and resistant that if we are left to ourselves, we will carry on exactly as the people did in 2 Chronicles 30:10, with "scorn and mockery."

Oh, how relevant and practical are the doctrines of God's sovereignty for our daily lives! If we did not know what Augustine knew, and what 2 Chronicles teaches us, how would we apply our wills and our assiduous efforts toward holiness and ministry without becoming self-reliant, self-exalting moralists? It is knowing that we must work out our salvation in such efforts, and that this effort is a gift of God's grace, that keeps us constant in our praying for enabling grace, and vigorous in our working (Philippians 2:12–13). How else could we say with the apostle Paul, "By the grace of God I am what I am, and his grace toward me was not in vain. On the contrary, I worked harder than any of them, though it was not I, but the grace of God that is with me"? (1 Corinthians 15:10). I worked hard, but it was not I. That is what 2 Chronicles and Augustine want us to learn.

Lord, I pray that You would fill us with
hope and joy and expectation
that You have the power to put Your hand on us,
and grant us the will to do what You command.
You have made it plain:
We are responsible to do what You tell us to do.
But we know that in ourselves we
do not have the will to do it.
And so we cry with Augustine,
"Lord, command what You will,
and give what You command."
Leave us not to ourselves. Have mercy.
In Jesus' name,
Amen.

Eight

ENDINGS ARE
FOR GRATITUDE,
BEGINNINGS ARE
FOR FAITH

The embrace may be only with the heart, or it may be with the arms, depending on proximity and the degree of the emotion. But in either case *gratitude* embraces a person with glad affections for *past* goodwill aimed at helping us; and *faith* embraces a person with glad affections for *future* promises aimed at helping us.

Since every moment is the beginning of the rest of your life, and every moment is the end of the past, every moment should be governed by the glad affections of both gratitude and faith.

Of course this is only possible if you see the world a certain way. If you see it the way biologist Richard Dawkins claims to see it, you will not experience your moments this way. Dawkins sees the world as a naturalist, that is, without God: "Like successful Chicago gangsters our genes have survived...in a highly competitive world,... [and so] a predominant quality to be expected in a successful gene is ruthless selfishness.... We are survival machines—robot vehicles programmed to preserve the selfish molecules known as genes" (from his book *The Selfish Gene,* quoted in a review by Phillip Johnson, *First Things* 97 [November 1999]: 70).

If you see the world that way, there are no persons to embrace, but only biological machines; no personal affections to feel, but only genetic programming; no goodwill in the past and no promises for the future, but only ruthless, blind, genetic "selfishness," that is, mindless survival of superior might.

But if you see the world the way Gustav Oehler (German Lutheran professor of Old Testament at Tübingen, 1812–1872) sees it, you will experience your moments differently. Oehler said, "It is clear that the Old Testament teaches a providence which embraces everything.... No sphere of chance exists in the Old Testament.... Even what men call accidental death is under God's direction [Exodus 21:12–13]" (*Theology of the Old Testament* [Minneapolis, MN: Klock and Klock Christian Publishers, 1978], 122).

In this view of things, looking back is looking on the past providence of God: "As for you, you meant evil against me, but God meant it for good" (Genesis 50:20). And looking forward is looking on the future providence of God: "The heart of man plans his way, but the LORD establishes his steps" (Proverbs 16:9). "Are not two sparrows sold for a penny? And not one of them will fall to the ground apart from your Father" (Matthew 10:29). "Surely goodness and mercy shall follow me all the days of my life" (Psalm 23:6).

If you see the world in this biblical way—and if you stand inside that biblical world as your humbly-accepted world—then every moment will be a point of gratitude toward the past and faith toward the future. The practical implications of this are great. For example, gratitude is one of the humblest affections; and faith is one of the boldest. Just think what kind of people we would be in the next year for the cause of Christ if we were continually humbled by our backward look of gratitude and continually emboldened by our forward look of faith! No, don't just think about it. Pursue it—with all your mind and all your heart.

Gracious Father, grant me a lowly spirit of gratitude.
Make me feel the preciousness of past grace.
Give me an honest memory of mercy.
Forgive me for the pride of unremembered
gifts and callous thanklessness.
Waken faith in my wavering soul
and give me strong confidence
in your solid promises.
Where past and future meet
make me humble and bold.
In Jesus' name
and for His sake,
Amen.

Nine

BOASTING IN MAN IS DOUBLY EXCLUDED

God loves it when man boasts in God, and God hates it when man boasts in man. "Let the one who boasts, boast in the Lord" (2 Corinthians 10:17). "Far be it from me to boast except in the cross of our Lord Jesus Christ" (Galatians 6:14). "The haughty looks of man shall be brought low, and the lofty pride of men shall be humbled, and the LORD alone will be exalted in that day. For the LORD of hosts has a day against all that is proud and lofty, against all that is lifted up" (Isaiah 2:11–12).

There are two reasons (at least) why God hates for man to boast in man. One is that boasting in man deflects man's attention from the Fountain of his joy and so ruins his life. It tricks man into replacing Magnificence with a mirror. Man was not made to admire man. He was made to admire God. The joy of admiration is prostituted and ruined when man tries to find galaxy-size Glory in the glow of his own reflection. God does not like the human damage done by boasting in man.

The other reason God hates for man to boast in man is this: It conveys the conviction that man is more admirable than God. Now that is, of course, untrue. But we would miss the point if we said: "God hates lying, and therefore God hates boasting in man because it conveys a lie." No. That's not quite right. What God hates is the dishonoring of God. Lying happens to be one way that He is dishonored as the God of truth. So the real problem with man's boasting in man is that it belittles God.

Boasting in God, on the other hand, does the double opposite: it honors God and gives man the joy for which he was made: admiring the infinitely admirable. Mercifully, therefore, God has doubly excluded boasting by the way He saves sinners.

First, boasting is excluded by faith. Romans 3:27, "Then what becomes of our boasting? It is excluded. By what kind of law? By a law of works? No, but by the law of faith." Why does faith exclude boasting? The reason is not merely because faith is a gift of God, which it is (Ephesians 2:8). But not all gifts exclude boasting in the same way. All the fruits of the Spirit are gifts of God—like love for people. But love for people is very different from faith in God's promises to help us love people. Love includes doing good things for people. This is virtuous action. But faith is different. Faith is unique among all the acts of the soul. It is the weakest and most helpless and most empty-handed. It is *all* dependence on Another. It is not the fruit of dependence as all the other virtues of the soul are. It is not the fruit of itself. In a sense, it is an acted non-act—an act that is entirely receiving. It is a doing, whose doing is the will to let another do all the doing.

I'll try to explain. I mean faith is an inclination of the soul to seek help from Christ with no expectation that any inclination of the soul is good enough to obtain help, not even the inclination of faith. It is unique among all the acts of the soul. Since it is empty-handed, it is not like a virtue. It looks to the virtue of another. It looks to the strength of another. It looks to the wisdom of another. It is entirely other-directed and other-dependent. Therefore, it can't boast in itself, for it can't even look at itself. It is the kind of thing that in a sense has no "self." As soon as the unique act of the soul exists, it is attached to Another from whom it gets all its reality.

Second, boasting is excluded by election. First Corinthians 1:27–29, "God *chose* [that is, *elected*] what is foolish in the world to shame the wise; God chose what is weak in the world to shame the strong; God chose what is low and despised in the world, even things that are not, to bring to nothing things that are, so that no human being might boast in the presence of God."

Notice the "so that." It signals the purpose of God's choosing. God's election is designed to remove boasting. The point is that God does not choose people with a view to any feature in us that would allow us to boast. In fact, Romans 9:11 makes clear that God's election is designed to make God's saving purpose rest finally on God alone, not any act of the human soul. "Though [Jacob and Esau] were not yet born and had done nothing either good or bad—in order that God's purpose of election might continue, not because of works but because of him who calls [God chose Jacob not Esau]." The contrast with works here is not faith, but "him who calls." The choice of God rests finally on God alone. He decides who will believe and undeservingly be saved.

Therefore, let us look away from ourselves and all human help. Let all boasting in man and man's accomplishments cease. "Let the one who boasts, boast in the Lord" (1 Corinthians 1:31).

*Dear Father, I confess with shame that
I am wired to love the praise of man.
I know this is sin, and deeply offensive
to Your infinite worth and beauty.
Forgive me, I pray, and make the truth of
Your election and Your faith-awakening
gift kill all vanity in me.
Set me, O Lord, not to brooding silence,
but to boasting in Your glorious name.
Through Christ I pray,
Amen.*

Ten

ALL WE WILL GET
IS MERCY

Let us make crystal clear at the beginning of each new day, all we will get from God as believers in Jesus is mercy. Whatever pleasures or pains may come our way in this day, they will all be mercy. This is why Christ came into the world—"in order that the Gentiles might glorify God for his mercy" (Romans 15:9). We were born again "according to his great mercy" (1 Peter 1:3); we pray daily "that we may receive mercy" (Hebrews 4:16); and we are now "waiting for the mercy of our Lord Jesus Christ that leads to eternal life" (Jude 1:21). If any Christian proves trustworthy, it is "by the Lord's mercy [he] is trustworthy" (1 Corinthians 7:25). In the end, when all is said and done, we will confess, "So then it depends not on human will or exertion, but on God, who has mercy" (Romans 9:16).

So as we face each day, let us humble ourselves and take the position of the blind man: "Jesus, Son of David, have mercy on me!" (Luke 18:38). Or the position of the leper: "Jesus, Master, have mercy on us" (Luke 17:13). And let us take heart that we will never obey God enough to put Him in debt to us. He will never owe us. "Who has given a gift to [God] that he might be repaid?" (Romans 11:35). And let us take heart that the smallest seed of true faith in Christ taps all the divine power of mercy—as the slightest touch of an electrical plug to the socket gets all the electricity.

Really? Did Jesus say that? He did. Consider.

In Luke 17:5, the apostles pleaded with the Lord, "Increase our faith!" And the Lord said, "If you had faith like a grain of mustard seed, you could say to this mulberry tree, 'Be uprooted and planted in the sea,' and it would obey you" (v. 6). In other words, the issue in your Christian life and ministry is not the strength or quantity of your faith, because that is not what uproots trees. God does. Therefore, the smallest faith that truly connects you with Christ will engage enough of His power for all you need. Moving trees is a small thing for Christ. The issue is not perfection for Christ, but connection to Christ. So take heart, the smallest seed of faith connects with all of Christ's mercy.

But what about your successes? When you succeed in obeying God, do you no longer need to be a supplicant of mercy? Jesus gives the answer in the next verses (Luke 17:7–10).

> Will any one of you who has a servant plowing or keeping sheep say to him when he has come in from the field, "Come at once and sit down at table"? Will he not rather say to him, "Prepare supper for me, and dress properly, and serve me while I eat and drink, and afterward you will eat and drink"? Does he thank the servant because he did what was commanded? So you also, when you have done all that you were commanded, say, "We are unworthy servants; we have only done what was our duty."

What does He mean that after doing all His commands we should still say, "We are unworthy servants"? He means, you never cease to be dependent on mercy. Doing all we are called to do does not make us deserving in relation to God. "Unworthy" after all obedience means humans cannot earn anything good from God. If we get it, it's mercy.

Therefore, I conclude, the fullest obedience and the smallest faith obtain the same thing from God: mercy. A mere mustard seed of faith taps into the mercy of tree-moving power. And flawless obedience leaves us utterly dependent on mercy. God may withhold some blessings of mercy for our good, if we stray from the path of growing faith. But even this withholding is another form of mercy.

The point is: Whatever the timing or form of God's mercy, we never rise above the status of beneficiaries of mercy. We are always utterly dependent on the undeserved. God never owes us anything in ourselves. The smallest faith and the fullest obedience receive one thing: almighty mercy.

Therefore let us humble ourselves and rejoice and "glorify God for His mercy"!

O Lord, forbid that I would be so foolish
as to be a lover of wages
more than a lover of undeserved rewards.
Make me feel the sweetness of being shown mercy.
Work childlikeness deeply into my soul,
and make me find my joy and my rest
in Your free gift of grace.
In Jesus' name,
Amen.

Eleven

A CALL FOR CORONARY CHRISTIANS

I am glad for adrenaline; I suspect it gets me through lots of Sundays. But it doesn't do much for Mondays. I am even more thankful for my heart. It just keeps on being a humble, quiet servant—during good days and bad days, happy and sad, high and low, appreciated and unappreciated. It never lets me down. It never says, "I don't like your attitude, Piper, I'm taking a day off." It just keeps humbly lubb-dubbing along.

Coronary Christians are like the heart in the causes they serve. Adrenal Christians are like adrenaline—a spurt of energy, and then fatigue. What the church and the world need today is marathoners, not just sprinters. People who find the pace to finish the (lifelong) race.

Oh, for coronary Christians! Christians committed to

great causes, not great comforts. I plead with you to dream a dream that is bigger than you and your families and your churches. Un-deify the American family, and say boldly that our children are not our cause; they are given to us to train for a cause. They are given to us for a short season so that we can train them for the great causes of truth and mercy and justice in a prejudiced, pain-filled, and perishing world.

My blood is boiling on this issue of rugged, never-say-die, coronary Christian commitment to great causes, because I've been brimming these days with the life of William Wilberforce. Now *there* was a coronary Christian in the cause of racial justice. He was deeply Christian, vibrantly evangelical, and passionately political in the House of Commons over the long haul in the fight against the African slave trade. On October 28, 1787, he wrote in his diary at the age of 28, "God Almighty has set before me two great objects, the suppression of the Slave Trade and the Reformation of [Morals]." In battle after battle in Parliament he was defeated, because "The Trade" was so much woven into the financial interests of the nation. But he never gave up and never sat down. He was coronary, not adrenal.

On February 24, 1807, at 4:00 A.M., twenty years later, the decisive vote was cast (Ayes, 283, Noes, 16) and the slave trade became illegal. The House rose almost to a man and turned towards Wilberforce in a burst of parliamentary cheers, while the little man with the curved spine sat, head bowed, tears streaming down his face (John Pollock, *Wilberforce*, 211).

The coronary Christian, William Wilberforce, never gave up. There were keys to his relentlessness. The greatness and the certainty and the rightness of the cause sustained him. Abolishing the slave trade was "the grand object of my Parliamentary existence."

"Before this great cause," he wrote in 1796, "all others dwindle in my eyes, and I must say that the certainty that I am right here, adds greatly to the complacency with which I exert myself in asserting it. If it please God to honor me so far, may I be the instrument of stopping such a course of wickedness and cruelty as never before disgraced a Christian country" (Pollock, 143).

He saw that adrenal spurts would never prevail: "I daily become more sensible that my work must be affected by constant and regular exertions rather than by sudden and violent ones" (Pollock, 116). He had learned the secret of being strengthened, not stopped, by opposition. One of his adversaries said, "He is blessed with a very sufficient quantity of that Enthusiastic spirit, which is so far from yielding that it grows more vigorous from blows" (Pollock, 105). Most of all, the secret of his coronary commitment to the great Cause was his radical allegiance to Jesus Christ.

He prayed—and may this prayer rouse many coronary lovers of Christ to fight racism, abortion, hunger, ignorance, poverty, homelessness, alcoholism, drug abuse, crime, corruption, violence, AIDS, apathy, unbelief...with unwavering perseverance—"[May God] enable me to have a single eye and a simple heart, desiring to please God, to do good to my fellow creatures and to testify my gratitude to my adorable Redeemer" (Pollock, 210).

Yes, Lord, yes! This is our heart's desire.
Forgive us for adrenaline spurts of righteousness.
Forgive us for little sprints of holiness.
Forgive us for short flashes of noble-minded sacrifice.
And build into the fiber of our faith
a rugged, resilient, never-say-die
perseverance in the cause of truth and love!
Make us coronary Christians!
In Jesus' name,
Amen.

Twelve

GOD IS NOT BORING

A Meditation on the Imagination

One of the great duties of the Christian mind is imagination. It is not the only thing the mind does. The mind observes. The mind analyzes and organizes. The mind memorizes. But imagination is different. It does not observe or analyze what we see; it imagines what we can't see, but what might really be there. Therefore it is very useful in science, because it helps turn up unseen explanations for things we don't understand, and leads to all kinds of discoveries. Or it imagines a new way of saying things that no one has said before, as in the case of creative writing and music and art.

I say that imagination is a Christian duty for two reasons. One is that you can't apply Jesus' golden rule without it. He said, "Whatever you wish that others would do to you, do also to them" (Matthew 7:12). We must imagine ourselves in their place and imagine what we would like done to us. Compassionate, sympathetic, helpful love hangs much on the imagination of the lover.

There are a thousand ways to say stupid and unhelpful things in a tense or tragic or joyful situation. How do we speak words that are "fitly chosen"? "A word fitly spoken is like apples of gold in a setting of silver" (Proverbs 25:11). One answer is that the Spirit of God gives us a "sympathetic imagination." "Sympathy" means we "feel with" someone. When we open our mouth, we spontaneously, with little reflection, imagine the right thing to say—or not to say—for the sake of others. Without imagination we would all be social klutzes.

The other reason I say that imagination is a Christian duty is that when a person speaks or writes or sings or paints about breathtaking truth in a boring way, it is probably a sin. The supremacy of God in the life of the mind is not honored when God and His amazing world are observed truly, analyzed duly, and communicated boringly. Imagination is the key to killing boredom. We must imagine ways to say truth for what it really is. And it is not boring.

God's world—all of it—rings with wonders. The imagination calls up new words, new images, new analogies, new metaphors, new illustrations, new connections to say old, glorious truth. Imagination is the faculty of the mind that God has given us to make the communication of His beauty beautiful.

Don't mistake what I am saying. Poets and painters and preachers don't make God's beauty more beautiful. They make it more visible. They cut through the dull fog of our finite, fallible, sin-distorted perception, and help us see God's beauty for what it really is. Imagination is like a telescope to the stars: It doesn't make them big. They are big without the telescope. It makes them look like what they are.

Imagination may be the hardest work of the human mind. And perhaps the most God-like. It is the closest we get to creation out of nothing. When we speak of beautiful truth, we must think of a pattern of words, perhaps a poem. We must conceive something that has never existed before and does not now exist in any human mind. We must think of an analogy or metaphor or illustration which has no existence. The imagination must exert itself to see it in our mind, when it is not yet there. We must create word combinations and music that have never existed before. All of this we do, because we are like God and because He is infinitely worthy of ever-new words and songs and pictures.

A college—or a church or a family—committed to the supremacy of God in the life of the mind will cultivate fertile imaginations. And, oh, how the world needs God-besotted minds that can say and sing and play and paint the great things of God in ways that have never been said or sung or played or painted before.

Imagination is like a muscle. It grows stronger when you flex it. And you must flex it. It does not usually put itself into action. It awaits the will. Imagination is also contagious. When you are around someone (alive or dead) who uses it a lot, you tend to catch it. So I suggest that you hang out with some people (mainly dead poets) who are full of imagination, and that you exert yourself to think up a new way to say an old truth. God is worthy. "Oh sing to the LORD a new song"—or picture, or poem, or figure of speech, or painting.

Dear God and Creator and Father,
I praise You for Your infinitely wise imagination!
I bow with wonder at Your power to put in place
the universe so full of marvels for our joy.
I pray for the grace of imagination,
lest I fail to love my fellow man
and fail to render Your glory
for what it really is,
most beautiful of all beauties.
Through Christ, I pray,
Amen.

Thirteen

THANKSGIVING FOR THE LIVES OF FLAWED SAINTS

God ordains that we gaze on His glory, dimly mirrored in the ministry of His flawed servants. He intends for us to consider their lives and peer through the imperfections of their faith and behold the beauty of their God. "Remember your leaders, those who spoke to you the word of God. Consider the outcome of their way of life, and imitate their faith" (Hebrews 13:7).

The God who fashions the hearts of all men (Psalm 33:15) means for their lives to display His truth and His worth. From Phoebe (Romans 16:1) to St. Francis, the divine plan holds firm. Paul spoke it over the life of the pagan Pharaoh: "For this very purpose I have raised you up, that I might show my power in you, and that my name might be proclaimed in all the earth" (Romans 9:17). From David the king, to David Brainerd the missionary, extraordinary and incomplete specimens of godliness and wisdom have kindled the worship of sovereign grace in the hearts of reminiscing saints. "Let this be recorded for a generation to come, so that a people yet to be created may praise the LORD" (Psalm 102:18).

The history of the world is a field strewn with broken stones, which are sacred altars designed to waken worship in the hearts of those who will take the time to read and remember. "I will remember the deeds of the LORD; surely I will remember Your wonders of old. I will meditate on all Your work and muse on Your deeds. Your way, O God, is holy; what god is great like our God?" (Psalm 77:11–13, NASB).

The aim of God's providence in the history of the world is worship flowing from the people of God. Ten thousand stories of grace and truth are meant to be remembered for the refinement of faith and the sustaining of hope and the guidance of love. "Whatever was written in former days was written for our instruction, that by steadfastness and by the encouragement of the scriptures we might have hope" (Romans 15:4, RSV). Those who nurture their hope by the history of grace will live their lives to the glory of God.

The lives of our flawed Christian heroes are inspiring

for two reasons: because they were flawed (like us) and because they were great (unlike us). Their flaws give us hope that maybe God could use us too. Their greatness inspires us to venture beyond the ordinary.

How does it come about that an ordinary person breaks out of the ruts of humdrum life to do something remarkable? It usually happens because of the inspiration of a man or woman they admire.

Do you have any heroes? Do you read about the lives of men and women who broke out of the mold and escaped the trap of the ordinary? Why not make a resolution now that you will read the biography of a Christian whom God made great. If you plan it, it is likely to happen. If you don't, it probably won't.

A few years ago, in preparation for our annual pastors' conference where I deliver a biographical address, I read *John G. Paton: Missionary to the New Hebrides*. It was worth all the hours even if only for one great paragraph. When Paton resolved to go to the unreached tribes of the South Sea Islands in 1856, a Christian gentleman objected, "You'll be eaten by cannibals!" To this Paton responded:

> Your own prospect is soon to be laid in the grave, there to be eaten by worms; I confess to you, that if I can but live and die serving and honoring the Lord Jesus, it will make no difference to me

whether I am eaten by Cannibals or by worms; and in the Great Day my resurrection body will arise as fair as yours in the likeness of our risen Redeemer. (p. 56)

This kind of abandon to the cause of Christ puts fire in my bones. If you don't know where to start, ask your pastor what biographies of Christians he would recommend. Or contact us at Desiring God for a list of the ones that have helped us.

*Thank You, Lord, for the lives of flawed
and faith-filled saints!
Thank You for grace, amazing grace,
that saves and uses sinners!
Lord, don't let us dream too small about our lives.
Don't let us limit Your power
by what we see in the mirror.
Help us to trust You. Help us,
as William Carey said,
to expect great things from God
and attempt great things for God.
We are not great. But You are great.
Your power is made perfect in our weakness.
We surrender all worldly claims on our lives.
Come. Make us useful for the glory of Christ.
In His great name, we pray,
Amen.*

Fourteen

WHY SATAN IS LEFT ON EARTH

Incentives to Battle for Joy in Jesus

Part of the problem of evil is the problem of why Satan is given so much freedom to harm the world, when God has the right and power to throw him in the pit. God will one day do away with Satan altogether (Revelation 20:3, 10). That will be no injustice to Satan. Nor would it be unjust for God to do it today. So why doesn't He, in view of how much misery Satan causes?

Satan roams around like a devouring lion seeking to destroy faith (1 Peter 5:8); he makes people sick and diseased (Acts 10:38); he tempts to sin (Luke 22:3–4); he blinds the minds of unbelievers (2 Corinthians 4:4); he takes people captive to do his will (2 Timothy 2:26); he kills (Revelation 2:10). One day God will stop him from doing this. Why doesn't He stop him now?

Could it be that there is a chance the devil and his angels will repent? Is God giving them time? No. The Bible teaches they are irredeemable. Jesus said that "the eternal fire...has been prepared for the devil and his angels" (Matthew 25:41, NASB). Jude confirms this when he says that the fallen angels are being "kept in eternal bonds under darkness for the judgment of the great day" (Jude 1:6, NASB).

Why then does God tolerate Satan? The key is that God aims to defeat Satan in a way that glorifies not only His power, but also the superior beauty and worth and desirability of His Son over Satan. God could simply exert raw power and snuff Satan out. That would glorify God's power. But it would not display so clearly the superior worth of Jesus over Satan. That will be displayed as Christ defeats Satan by His death and then by winning allegiance from the saints because of His superior truth and beauty above the ugliness and lies of Satan.

Central to this plan is that God defeats Satan in stages through the work of Christ. First, we were forgiven all our trespasses by Christ's death on the cross. Paul said that in doing this God "disarmed the rulers and authorities and put them to open shame, by triumphing over them in him" (Colossians 2:15).

This was the first stage of Satan's defeat. The lethal weapon of soul-destroying sin and guilt is taken out of

Satan's hand. He is disarmed of the single weapon that can condemn us—unforgiven sin. We see this in 1 Corinthians 15:55–57, "O death, where is your victory? O death, where is your sting? The sting of death is sin, and the power of sin is the law. But thanks be to God, who gives us the victory through our Lord Jesus Christ." What makes the sting of death powerful, that is, eternally lethal, is sin. The law sees to it that sin gets a just condemnation: eternal judgment. That is Satan's weapon: unforgiven sin, reinforced by the sanctions of the law. But if our sins could be forgiven, Satan could not condemn us. And, indeed, they are forgiven through faith in God's grace bought by the blood of Jesus.

Without sin and law to condemn us, Satan is a defeated foe. He is disarmed. Christ has triumphed over him, not yet by casting him into hell and nullifying his influence on earth, but by letting him live and watch while millions of saints find forgiveness for their sins and turn their back on Satan because of the greater glory of Christ.

That is the second stage of defeat: not only what happened on the cross for sinners, but what happens in the hearts of those who are saved—the conversion of people by the power of the gospel of the cross. Jesus says to Paul that his mission to the Gentiles is "to open their eyes, so that they may turn from...the power of Satan to God" (Acts 26:18). This is what happens when God removes the blindness caused by the devil and gives us the light of the gospel of the glory of Christ (2 Corinthians 4:4–6). This enables people to see the ugliness of Satan and the beauty of Christ, so that their choosing Christ glorifies not only God's power, but Christ's superior beauty and worth over Satan.

This way of defeating Satan is more costly than just snuffing him out. Christ suffered for this triumph and the world suffers. But God's values are not so easily reckoned. If Christ obliterated all demons now (which He could do), His sheer power would be seen as glorious, but His superior beauty and worth would not shine so brightly as when God's people renounce the promises of Satan, trust in Christ's blood and righteousness, and take pleasure in the greater glory of Jesus over Satan.

This means that our treasuring Christ above all the promises of sin and Satan is part of the triumph that God designs for this age. Therefore, take up arms and defeat the devil by being bold and glad in the superior glory of the Son of God! I do not say it is easy. It is very costly. The path of love that leads from the cross of Christ to the glory of Christ is a road of sacrifice. Christ's superior beauty over Satan and sin is seen best when we are willing to suffer because we have tasted it and want to share it. One of the greatest blows against the power of darkness comes from the blood of martyrs. "They have conquered him [Satan!] by the blood of the Lamb and by the word of their testimony, for they loved not their lives even unto death" (Revelation 12:11).

O Lord, Your ways are not our ways,
and Your thoughts are not our thoughts.
Yours are unsearchable and often
baffling to our finite minds.
You have chosen to give Satan freedom to do
great damage, when it would be no injustice
to him to destroy him now.
We bow before Your wisdom.
We embrace with Jesus the cross that saves
our souls and sends us into battle with faith
in the superior beauty and worth of Christ.
Go with us. Help us.
In His great name,
Amen.

Fifteen

The Path of Wisdom May Not Be the Most Fruitful Path for God's Glory

We are held accountable for being wise not influential.

The powers of our mind are simply not adequate for deciding which path of life will be most effective for God's kingdom purposes to save sinners, and transform lives, and exalt His name. The reason is that all the signs that we can see may point to a very fruitful ministry in one direction that fits our gifts and seems to meet the greatest need and seems to be a God-given opportunity at this particular moment, and gets confirmation from wise counselors, and seems to be part of a pattern of divinely orchestrated circumstances, and *yet*, in spite of all that wisdom, another path than the one that seemed so fruitful, may lead to a single seemingly insignificant event that you could have never foreseen or planned, but which God uses to bring about an effect for the glory of His name beyond anything the wise path would have produced.

For example, what if all the evidences pointed the southern preacher, Mordecai Fowler Ham, away from an evangelistic crusade in Charlotte, North Carolina, in September 1934? What if Scripture and prayer and counsel and circumstances all pointed to a larger, more fruitful ministry in Atlanta? If Mordecai Ham, who has been virtually forgotten by the world, had gone to Atlanta instead of Charlotte, the sixteen-year old William Franklin Graham would not have been converted under his preaching. But, as it happened, in the providence of God, Billy Graham became a Christian because Mordecai Ham came to Charlotte. That conversion was perhaps the most fruitful moment of Ham's entire ministry. No human can plan such things. And no human wisdom can see them coming.

So then what becomes of all our planning and all our strategic thinking? Clearly our planning does not render the last word on the fruitfulness of our lives. We simply do not know whether one path or the other will prove to be the path on which some remarkable turn of affairs may take place for the glory of God all out of proportion to what we planned or expected. A seemingly useless path may prove more effective than the best plan we could have made. You simply cannot know what God may do on any given path of faithfulness.

What conclusion can we draw from this observation? We should *not* draw the conclusion that thinking and planning about what is "wise" is a waste of time or is the wrong way to make decisions. If we abandon wisdom, thinking there is no way we can know the most effective path for our life, then we contradict the whole teaching of Scripture that it is good to be wise and to pursue wisdom.

But human wisdom is not omniscience. Wisdom does not equal knowing for sure that the path chosen will be the most fruitful path. Wisdom means doing the best you can with all the resources at your disposal to discern what the path of fruitfulness is for the glory of God.

This means that we are going to be held responsible by God to make our choices wisely, because that shows that in this moment our heart is obedient to God's Word and desirous of His glory. *That* is what we are held accountable for. But we are *not* responsible that the choices we make, with the best motives and knowledge available, and with good counsel, will prove to be the most influential or effective choices in producing converts or changing lives. That is God's work, not ours.

We will be called to account at the last day for whether

we have sought wisdom in reliance on God's Spirit and for the glory of God's Son. We will not be held accountable for whether our planning resulted in wonderful, serendipitous events like the conversion of a Billy Graham.

So what effect, then, should this observation have on our efforts to act wisely? It should at least give us an intense passion to honor God in *this* moment of decision-making. It should make us more zealous in this moment for God's glory to be shown in how we make decisions, not how they turn out. And then we should have a deep peace that the final effectiveness of our lives does not hang on our wisdom, but on God's sovereignty.

God will make it His rule to use our best efforts at wise, God-honoring choices to produce the most influential life. But not always. He can break that rule and make even a foolish decision fruitful. He has His ways to keep us humble and fearful of pride. He has his ways to keep us hopeful and protected from discouragement in view of our fallibility. We should be emboldened to move and act in faith, even if we think that our present choice may not have all the data possible, or all the counsel possible, or all the thought and prayer possible.

Our sovereign God is able to take the 80-percent-wise choice and make it more influential for Christ than the 90-percent-wise choice. This should not make us cavalier about the pursuit of wisdom, since we will be held accountable to pursue it, but it should make us bold that our wisdom is not what determines our influence or our fruitfulness in the end. God is. And He can take the worst detour and, for His wise and sometimes inscrutable purposes, make that route the most fruitful, even though we, in our folly, may be disciplined for taking it.

O God, You are all-wise and sovereign.
Therefore we thank You for keeping
in Your hands, not ours,
the final determination of which paths
are influential for Christ in our lives.
We confess our sin and our fallibility.
We do not want to run the world.
We want You to run it.
We rejoice that our best efforts
may yield modest fruit.
And our most foolish choices may be
made the means of great fruit.
In Jesus' name,
Amen.

Sixteen

STORMS ARE THE TRIUMPH OF HIS ART

John Newton wrote "Amazing Grace" after God saved him from a life—as he says—of being "a wretch" on the high seas for thirteen years. Then he became a pastor who faithfully loved two flocks for forty-three years in Olney and then in London, England.

Newton was a great and tender warrior against despair in other people's lives. He had been so hopeless and so beyond recovery in his sin that his own salvation constantly amazed him. If anyone should have despaired it was he. But God saved him. On March 21, 1748 a storm at sea wakened him from his folly. From that night at age twenty-three to the year he died at age eighty-two, he marked the day of his awakening on board the *Greyhound* with fasting and prayer and thankful rededication of his life to Jesus. As an old man he wrote, "The 21st in March is a day much to be remembered by me, and I have never suffered it to pass wholly unnoticed since the year 1748. On that day the Lord sent from on high, and delivered me out of the deep waters" (*Works*, I, 26–7).

He wrote his own epitaph to capture the wonder of his conversion and his undeserved ministry:

> JOHN NEWTON, Clerk, Once an Infidel and Libertine, A Servant of Slaves in Africa, Was, by the rich mercy of our Lord and Savior JESUS CHRIST, Preserved, restored, pardoned, And appointed to preach the Faith He had long labored to destroy, Near 16 years at Olney in Bucks; And...years in this church. (*Works*, I, 90)

Newton's amazing rescue from utter wretchedness and hardness of heart and blaspheming made him a rescuer of hopeless people all the rest of his life. His first biographer and friend, Richard Cecil, closes his memoir of Newton by pleading with young people:

> Mark the error of despair. We should see that the case of a praying man cannot be desperate—that if a man be out of the pit of hell, he is on the ground of mercy. We should recollect that God sees a way of escape when we see none—that nothing is too

hard for him—that he warrants our dependence, and invites us to call on him in the day of trouble, and gives a promise of deliverance. (*Works*, I, 126)

Newton had a favorite poet who died almost a hundred years before Newton was born. His name was George Herbert. He was born in 1593 into a wealthy Welsh family, lost his father when he was three, became a "public orator" in 1620 and a member of Parliament in 1625. But in 1630 he gave it all away to become a simple parish pastor in Bemerton. For the rest of his life he loved and served a flock as Newton did. Newton loved Herbert's poetry. Small wonder, when you read this verse from his poem "The Bag." They were both enthralled with amazing grace that banishes hopelessness from the sinner's heart. Herbert's poem captures Newton's message and life:

Away, Despair! My gracious Lord doth hear:
Though winds and waves assault my keel,
He doth preserve it: he doth steer,
Ev'n when the boat seems most to reel:
Storms are the triumph of his art:
Well may he close his eyes, but not his heart.
(Works, I, 128)

It was certainly true in Newton's case: God's storm was a triumphant art of grace. For a season, God's face may turn away from His chosen ones, but not His heart. So let us learn from John Newton and George Herbert to say, "Away, Despair!" Let us embrace the precious truth of Jesus' words, "It is not those who are well who need-a-physician, but those who are sick. I have not come to call the righteous but sinners to repentance" (Luke 5:31–32, NASB). There is no condemnation to those who are in Christ Jesus. Listen as Paul adds, "It is a trustworthy statement, deserving full acceptance, that Christ Jesus came into the world to save sinners, among whom I am foremost" (1 Timothy 1:15, NASB). And finally, to double our hope, give heed to Hebrews 6:18, "By two unchangeable things in which it is impossible for God to lie, we who have taken refuge would have strong encouragement to take hold of the hope set before us" (NASB).

O Lord of hope, give us the eyes of
John Newton and George Herbert.
Give us eyes to see the utter unlikeliness
of being loved by Christ.
Take away the feeling that we deserve happiness.
Cause us to be amazed at the wonder of grace.
May grumbling and murmuring depart from our lips,
O Lord, and make us tender toward sinners.
Thank You, Father, for mercy.
We cherish Your kindness
and long to give to others
the way You have given to us.
In Jesus' name,
Amen.

Seventeen

THE VALUE OF LEARNING HISTORY

A Lesson from Jude

The little New Testament letter of Jude teaches us something about the value of learning history. This is not the main point of the letter. But it is real and striking.

In this next-to-last book of the Bible, Jude writes to encourage the saints to "contend earnestly for the faith which was once for all handed down to the saints" (verse 3, NASB). The letter is a call to vigilance in view of "certain persons [who] have crept in unnoticed...ungodly persons who turn the grace of our God into licentiousness and deny our only Master and Lord, Jesus Christ" (verse 4). Jude describes these folks in vivid terms. They "revile the things which they do not understand" (verse 10). They "are grumblers, finding fault, following after their own lusts; they speak arrogantly, flattering people for the sake of gaining an advantage" (verse 16). They "cause divisions, [and are] worldly-minded, devoid of the Spirit" (verse 19).

This is a devastating assessment of people who are not outside the church but have "crept in unnoticed." Jude wants them to be spotted for who they really are, so that the church is not deceived and ruined by their false teaching and immoral behavior.

One of his strategies is to compare them to other persons and events in history. For example, he says that "Sodom and Gomorrah...since they in the same way as these indulged in gross immorality and went after strange flesh, are exhibited as an example in undergoing the punishment of eternal fire" (verse 7). So Jude compares these people to Sodom and Gomorrah. His point in doing this is to say that Sodom and Gomorrah are "an example" of what will happen when people live like these intruders are living. So, in Jude's mind, knowing the history of Sodom and Gomorrah is very useful in helping detect such error and deflect it from the saints.

Similarly in verse 11, Jude piles up three other references to historical events as comparisons with what is happening in his day among Christians. He says "Woe to them! For they have gone the way of Cain, and for pay they have rushed headlong into the error of Balaam, and perished in the rebellion of Korah." This is remarkable. Why refer to three different historical incidents like this that happened thousands of years earlier—Genesis 19 (Sodom), Genesis 3 (Cain), Numbers 22–24 (Balaam), Numbers 16 (Korah)? What's the point?

Here are three points:

1. Jude assumes that the readers know these stories! Is that not amazing? This was the first century! No books in anyone's homes. No Bibles available. No story tapes. Just oral instruction for almost all the common people. And he assumed that they would know "the way of Cain" and "the error of Balaam" and "the rebellion of Korah"? Do you know these stories? This is astonishing! He expects them to know these things. Surely, then, the standards of Bible knowledge in the church today are too low.

2. Jude assumes that knowing this history will illumine the present situation. The Christians will handle the error better today if they know similar situations from yesterday. In other words, history is valuable for Christian living. To know that Cain was jealous and hated his brother and resented his true spiritual communion with God will alert you to watch for such things even among brothers. To know that Balaam finally caved in and made the Word of God a means of worldly gain makes you better able to spot that sort of thing. To know that

Korah despised legitimate authority and resented Moses' leadership will protect you from factious folk who dislike anyone being seen as their leader.

3. Is it not clear, then, that God ordains for events to happen and be recorded as history, so that we will know them and become wiser and more insightful in this present time for the sake of Christ and His church?

Therefore never debunk history. Never scorn the past. Never stop learning from the providence of God and what He has put forward as our lesson book. Knowing history will increase the urgency and preciousness of our present life, because it will make this life look very short against the unrelenting flow of centuries. That is a good lesson to learn. Life is a vapor. Anything to help us see this will make us wiser: "Teach us to number our days that we may get a heart of wisdom" (Psalm 90:12). Gain some knowledge of the past every day. And let us give ourselves and our children one of the best protections against the folly of the future, namely, a knowledge of the past.

"Lord, You have been our dwelling
place in all generations.
Before the mountains were brought forth,
or ever You had formed the earth and the world,
from everlasting to everlasting You are God."
But we are like grass:
we flourish for a moment and then wither.
We are like a vapor:
we appear from the mouth,
and two seconds later we are gone.
Give us a mind to know the past,
lest we waste our fleeting lives
repeating its mistakes.
In Jesus' never-changing name,
Amen.

Eighteen

ALREADY: *DECISIVELY AND IRREVOCABLY FREE; NOT YET: FINALLY AND PERFECTLY FREE*

Romans 6 and 7 teaches that, when we trust in Christ as our Savior and Lord and Treasure of our lives, we are united to Christ (Romans 6:5; 7:4). In this union with Christ we die (Romans 6:8; Colossians 2:20; 3:3) and rise again (Romans 6:4; Colossians 2:12; Ephesians 2:6). Therefore a decisive and irrevocable new creation comes into being (2 Corinthians 5:17), and a decisive and irrevocable liberation happens (Romans 6:14, 18). We pass from death to (eternal!) life. Our decisive judgment is behind us—at Golgotha (John 5:24). We have moved from the dominion of darkness into the kingdom of God's Son (Colossians 1:13).

But we also learn from these chapters that our liberation from sin is not yet final and perfect. Decisive and irrevocable, yes! But final and perfect, no! Sin still dwells within us (Romans 7:17, 20). Evil is present in us (Romans 7:21). The "flesh" is a daily troubler of our souls (Romans 7:25). We are not yet perfect, nor have we already obtained our crown and prize (Philippians 3:12). We are liars if we say we have no sin (1 John 1:8, 10).

How then does the apostle Paul teach us to live? Will he say: "You are decisively and irrevocably new, so you can coast through life with no fight to become new?" Or will he say, "You are not decisively and irrevocably new and must therefore fight to get to that place in Christ?" No, neither of these. He will say: By faith, embrace all that God is for you in Christ and all that you are for His glory in Christ. Believe that. And now, with that confidence, fight to take possession of the territory that Christ has conquered for you. Fight to become in practice what you are in Christ. Here are eight illustrations of this truth:

1. *Statement of newness:* Romans 6:14, "Sin shall not be master over you, for you are not under law but under grace."

Command to become new: Romans 6:12, "Do not let sin reign in your mortal body."

2. *Statement of newness:* Romans 6:18, "Having been freed from sin, you became slaves of righteousness."
Command to become new: Romans 6:19, "Present your members as slaves to righteousness."

3. *Statement of newness:* Romans 6:6, "Our old self was crucified with Him."
Command to become new: Romans 6:11, "Consider yourselves to be dead to sin."

4. *Statement of newness:* Colossians 3:9, "You laid aside the old self with its evil practices."
Command to become new: Ephesians 4:22, "Lay aside the old self, which is being corrupted in accordance with the lusts of deceit."

5. *Statement of newness:* Colossians 3:10, "[You] have put on the new self who is being renewed to a true knowledge according to the image of the One who created him."
Command to become new: Ephesians 4:24, "Put on the new self, which in the likeness of God has been created in righteousness and holiness of the truth."

6. *Statement of newness:* Galatians 3:27, "All of you who were baptized into Christ have clothed your-selves with Christ."

   Command to become new: Romans 13:14, "But put on the Lord Jesus Christ."

7. *Statement of newness:* Galatians 5:24, "Those who belong to Christ Jesus have crucified the flesh with its passions and desires."

   Command to become new: Romans 13:14, "Make no provision for the flesh in regard to its lusts."

8. *Statement of newness:* 1 Corinthians 5:7, "Just as you are in fact unleavened."

   Command to become new: 1 Corinthians 5:7, "Clean out the old leaven so that you may be a new lump [of dough]."

Knowing this and learning how to walk with confidence (because of our newness) and with urgency (because of the demand to become new) is the secret of the Christian life. This is the way the apostle Paul lived. He expressed it like this: "Not that I have already obtained this or am already perfect, but I press on to make it my own, because Christ Jesus has made me his own" (Philippians 3:12). Already Christ's own. But pressing on to make it his own.

God's will for us is not paralyzing frustration because of imperfection. His will is liberating courage because of the certainty of our future in Him. The Not Yet makes us humble and vigilant. And sometimes the road seems long. But the Already makes us confident and bold, and reminds us that the road is short. Jesus walked it. And in Him, we are already home. While we live, this is our calling: brokenhearted boldness. Contrite confidence. The image of Christ on earth: the Lion and the Lamb.

O Lord, this is our heart's desire:
Make us meek, and make us mighty.
Give us confidence in the finished work of Christ,
and give us humility because
we are so far from perfection.
Open our eyes to the wonder of what
you have already done.
And forbid that we would claim
more now than is true.
We are weak, we are sinful,
and we need Your help.
Thank You for our permanent acceptance in Christ.
Thank You for our daily help from Christ.
Thank You for laying hold on us.
Now complete the work You have begun.
In Jesus' name, we pray,
Amen.

Nineteen

IF YOU WANT TO LOVE, YOU MUST DIE TO THE LAW

If you want to be a loving person, the way to pursue it is to die to the Law and to pursue a vital, all-satisfying union with Christ. Romans 7:4 says, "You also have died to the law through the body of Christ, so that you may belong to another, to him who has been raised from the dead, in order that we may bear fruit for God." Notice the exchange: die to the law and belong to the one who was raised from the dead, that is, Jesus. This leads, Paul says, to bearing fruit for God. And the preeminent fruit of the Christian life is love. Therefore the key to love is to die to the law and embrace Jesus Christ by faith as the Savior and Treasure of your life.

But this does not mean that the Law aimed at something other than love. Romans 13:10 says, "Love is the fulfillment of the law" (NASB). So it seems that death to the Law means something like: Stop using the Law unlawfully. That's the way Paul talks in 1 Timothy 1. There are folks who want to be "teachers of the Law" but "they do not understand...what they are saying" (verse 7). What are they doing wrong?

Paul explains in 1 Timothy 1:5 that "the goal of our instruction is love from a pure heart and a good conscience and a sincere faith." So Paul's gospel ministry aims at the fruit of love. People who love from "sincere faith" are in sync with the gospel.

Where does this love come from? He says it comes "from a pure heart and a good conscience and a sincere faith." In other words, the way to pursue love is by focusing on the transformation of the *heart* and the *conscience* and the awakening and strengthening of *faith*. Love is not pursued first or decisively by focusing on a list of behavioral commandments and striving to conform to them. That is what we must die to.

Then in 1 Timothy 1:6–7, Paul describes some men who don't understand this and yet are trying to use the Law for moral transformation. They are making a mess of it. He says, "Some men, straying from these things [that is, from heart, the conscience, and faith], have turned aside to fruitless discussion, wanting to be teachers of the Law, even though they do not understand...what they are saying." So their error is a misuse of the Law. They are trying to teach the Law, but they are turning aside from matters of the heart and conscience and faith. And so they are not arriving at love.

Is then the Law at fault? No. Paul absolves the Law, by saying in 1 Timothy 1:8, "But we know that the Law is good, if one uses it lawfully." The "lawful" use of the Law is to use it as a pointer to the gospel of the risen Christ, which awakens love. Paul confirms this in verse 9 by saying, "Law is not made for a righteous person, but for those who are lawless, rebellious, for the ungodly and sinners." What does he mean? He means that the Law does not need to do its job for those who are united to Christ by faith and are bearing the fruit of love. It needs to do its job by confronting sinners with the fact that their lives are contrary to the gospel and that they must pursue "the gospel of the glory of the blessed God" and belong to the one who was raised from the dead.

Paul says, with a sweeping statement in verses 10–11, that the Law is for pointing out, and convicting people of, "whatever is contrary to sound teaching, according to the glorious gospel of the blessed God." This is very significant. Notice the connection between the Law and the gospel here. Who is the Law for? It is for "the lawless, rebellious, the ungodly and sinners," that is, for those whose lives are not "according to the glorious gospel." That is, for those who do not love. For love is the aim of Paul's gospel (verse 5). The point is that the Law does not produce lives that accord with the gospel. The *gospel* produces lives that accord with the gospel. Used lawfully, the law sends us to the gospel. That's the point of Romans 7:4 — you must die to the Law [as a way of producing the fruit of love] and be united to Christ by faith "so that you might bear the fruit [of love] for God."

In other words, according to 1 Timothy 1:5–11, the Law is meant to accuse and convict people of breaking the gospel! "The law is for…whatever is contrary to…the glorious gospel" (verses 10–11). The law of commandments is not the first and decisive means of fruit-bearing for the Christian. Rather the Law brings us to Christ so that, as Romans 7:4 says, "you might be joined to…Him who was raised from the dead, in order that we might bear fruit [of love] for God." Oh let us embrace the risen Christ!

Life is too brief to waste it romancing the Law of commandments. That marriage will not bear the offspring of love. Make haste to Christ. Let the Law be, not the wife, but the humble matchmaker between you and Jesus. Don't fall in love with, and don't hate, the humble go-between. Die to the Law. Belong to the living Christ.

Open the eyes of our hearts, Father,
to see the precious and limited role of Your Law
in bearing the fruit of love in our lives.
Lead us into deep and personal union with Jesus.
Let this relationship with the living Christ
transform our minds and wills
so that we want what He wants
and hate what He hates.
Make us, by this union,
radically loving people.
In Jesus' name, we pray,
Amen.

Twenty

HOW OPEN THEISM
HELPS US CONCEAL OUR
HIDDEN IDOLATRIES

Bad theology hurts people and dishonors God. Open Theism is bad theology. It is a newer movement that says, "God can't foreknow the good or bad decisions of the people He creates until He creates these people and they, in turn, create their decisions" (Greg Boyd, *Letters from a Skeptic* [Chariot Victor Publishing: Colorado Springs, 1994], 30). In other words, God's foreknowledge is limited—massively limited. Thomas Oden says of this new view, "The fantasy that God is ignorant of the future is a heresy that must be rejected on scriptural grounds" (Thomas Oden, "The Real Reformers and the Traditionalists," *Christianity Today* [9 February 1998]: 46). A theology so seriously flawed will hurt people and dishonor God in more ways than anyone can foresee. Consider only one way.

Open Theism may help conceal deep idolatry in the soul. One of the great needs of our souls is to know if we treasure anything on earth more than we treasure Christ. Treasuring anyone or anything more than Christ is idolatry. Paul said in Colossians 3:5, "Put to death therefore what is earthly in you...*covetousness,* which is *idolatry.*" If covetousness is idolatry, then desiring earthly things more than we desire God is idolatry. That means we must be more satisfied in Christ and His wisdom than we are in all our relationships and accomplishments and possessions on earth.

Now how does Open Theism help us conceal from ourselves the idolatries in our souls? It ascribes *ultimate* causality for many calamities and evils to Satan or the autonomous will of man, not finally to the all-disposing counsel and wisdom of God above and behind Satan. For example, Boyd says:

> When an individual inflicts pain on another individual, I do not think we can go looking for "the purpose of God" in the event.... I know Christians frequently speak about "the purpose of God" in the midst of a tragedy caused by someone else.... But this I regard to simply be a piously confused way of thinking. (*Letters from a Skeptic*, 47)

Similarly, John Sanders writes:

> God does not have a specific divine purpose for each and every occurrence of evil.... When a two-month-old child contracts a painful, incurable bone cancer that means suffering and death, it is pointless evil. The Holocaust is pointless evil. The rape and dismemberment of a young girl is pointless evil. The accident that caused the death of my brother was a tragedy. God does not have a specific purpose in mind for these occurrences. (*The God Who Risks* [Downers Grove, Ill.: InterVarsity Press, 1998], 262)

If not "the purpose of God," what then is ultimate? Either man's will, which is ultimately "self-determining" and can even surprise God (as Open Theists believe), or the will of an evil spirit which is also ultimately "self-determining." For example, after admitting that "God can sometimes use the evil wills of personal beings, human or divine, to his own ends," Boyd then says, "This by no means entails that there is a divine will behind every activity of an evil spirit" (*God at War* [Downers Grove, Ill.: InterVarsity Press, 1997], 154, cf. 57, 141). "A self-determining, supremely evil being rules the world" (54). "The *ultimate* reason behind all evil in the world is found in Satan, not God" (54, my italics).

How does this worldview help us conceal the idolatry of our soul? It works like this. Open Theism denies that God is the final, purposive disposer of all things (Job 2:10; Amos 3:6; Rom. 8:28; Eph. 1:11). Therefore it asserts that God's wisdom does not hold final sway (Rom. 11:33–36), and thus God is not fulfilling a plan for our good in all our miseries (Jeremiah 29:11; 32:40). Open Theism implies, therefore, that we should not think about the wisdom of God's purpose in causing or permitting our calamities. In other words, Open Theism discourages us from asking what sanctifying purpose God may have in ordaining that our misery come about.

But in reality our pain and losses are always a test of how much we treasure the all-wise, all-governing God in comparison to what we have lost. We see this merciful testing of God throughout the Scriptures. For example, in Deuteronomy 8:3 Moses said, "And [God] humbled you and let you hunger and fed you with manna, which you did not know, nor did your fathers know, that he might make you know that man does not live by bread alone, but man lives by every word that comes from the mouth of the LORD." In other words, God ordains the hard times ("he...let you hunger") to see if we have made a god out of our good times. Do we love bread, or do we love God? Do we treasure God and trust His good purposes in pain, or do we love His gifts more and get angry when He takes them away?

We see this testing in Psalm 66:10–12, "For you, O God, have tested us; you have tried us as silver is tried. You brought us into the net; you laid a crushing burden on our backs; you let men ride over our heads; we went through fire and through water." And we see it in the life of Paul. When he prayed for his thorn in the flesh to be taken away, Christ told him what God's purpose in the pain was. "Three times I pleaded with the Lord about this, that it should leave me. But He said to me, 'My grace is sufficient for you, for my power is made perfect in weakness'" (2 Corinthians 12:8–9). The test for Paul was: Will you value the magnifying of Christ's power more than a pain-free life?

We see this testing in 1 Peter 1:6–7: "In this you rejoice, though now for a little while, as was necessary, you have been grieved by various trials, so that the tested genuineness of your faith—more precious than gold that perishes though it is tested by fire—may be found to result in praise and glory and honor at the revelation of Jesus Christ." God ordains trials to refine our faith and prove that we really trust His wisdom and grace and power when hard times come. Similarly in James 1:2–3, 12, "Count it all joy, my brothers, when you meet trials of various kinds, for you know that the testing of your faith produces steadfastness.... Blessed is the man who remains steadfast under trial, for when he has stood the test he will receive the crown of life, which God has promised to those who love him." Do we love God? That is the point of the test. Do we cherish Him and the merciful wisdom of His painful purposes more than we cherish pain-free lives? That is the point of God's testing.

Our trials reveal the measure of our affection for this earth—both its good things and bad things. Our troubles expose our latent idolatry.

For those who believe that God rules purposefully and wisely over all things, our response to loss is a signal of how much idolatry is in our souls. Do we really treasure what we have lost more than God and His wisdom? If we find ourselves excessively angry or resentful or bitter, it may well show that we love God less that what we lost. This is a very precious discovery, because it enables us to repent and seek to cherish Christ as we ought, rather than being deceived into thinking all is well.

But Open Theism denies that God always has a wise purpose in our calamities ("God does not have a specific divine purpose for each and every occurrence of evil"), and so it obscures the test of our idolatrous hearts. Open Theism does not encourage us to see or savor the merciful designs of God in our pain. It teaches that there is either no design or that the design of the evil done against us is ultimately owing to Satan or evil men ("The ultimate reason behind all evil in the world is found in Satan, not God").

Therefore, we may be so angry with Satan and with evil people (which is legitimate up to a point), that we fail to ask whether our anger reflects an excessive attachment to what we just lost. But if, contrary to Open Theism, we must reckon with the fact that God's wisdom is the ultimate reason we lost our earthly treasure, then we will be forced to do the very valuable act of testing our hearts to see if we loved something on earth more than the wisdom of God in taking it from us.

All of life is meant to reflect the infinite value of Christ (Philippians 1:20). We show His infinite worth by treasuring Him above all things and all persons. Believing in His all-ruling, all-wise sovereignty helps reveal our idolatries in times of pain and loss. Not believing that God has a wise purpose for every event helps conceal our idolatries. Thus Open Theism, against all its conscious designs, tends to undermine a means of grace that our deceptive hearts need.

Gracious, all-knowing Father,
we praise You for Your infinite wisdom,
and for Your wise and holy purposes that
govern all You do, and all You permit to be done.
We rejoice and take heart from the precious
truth that nothing befalls us but by Your
loving will toward us Your children.
We pray that You will protect Your church
from harmful error, and lead Your flock
in the path of truth.
Expose our idols, O God.
And grant us to treasure Christ
above all things.
In His name, we pray,
Amen.

Twenty-One

HOW TO QUERY GOD

Thoughts on Romans 9:19–20

You will say to me then, "Why does he still find fault? For who can resist his will?" But who are you, O man, to answer back to God? Will what is molded say to its molder, "Why have you made me like this?"

Clearly Paul was displeased with this response to his teaching about God. Does this mean that it's always wrong to ask questions in response to biblical teaching? I don't think so.

Paul had said some controversial things. Peter admitted that Paul's letters were sometimes hard to understand: "There are some things in them that are hard to understand, which the ignorant and unstable twist to their own destruction, as they do the other Scriptures" (2 Peter 3:16). Paul had said that God "has mercy on whom he wills and hardens whom he wills" (Romans 9:18). The point was: God himself decides finally whether we are hard-hearted or not. "Before they were born or do anything good or evil" God had mercy on Jacob and gave Esau over to hardness (Romans 9:11–13).

Someone hears this and objects in verse 19, "Why does he still find fault? For who can resist his will?" To this Paul responds, "You, a mere human being, have no right to answer back to God."

The word "answer back" (*antapokrinomenos*) occurs one other time in the New Testament, namely, in Luke 14:5–6. Jesus is showing the lawyers that it is lawful to heal on the Sabbath. He said to them, "'Which of you, having a son or an ox that has fallen into a well on a Sabbath day, will not immediately pull him out?' And they could not answer back (*antapokrithēnai*) to these things."

In what sense could they not "answer back"? They could not show Him wrong. They could not legitimately criticize Him. They could not truly contradict what He said. So the word "answer back" probably carries the meaning: "answer back with a view to criticizing or disagreeing or correcting."

That, I think, is what displeased Paul in Romans 9:20. This leaves open the possibility that a different kind of question would be acceptable, namely, a humble, teachable question that wants to understand more, if possible, but not rebuke or condemn or criticize what has been said.

For example, in Luke 1:31 the angel Gabriel comes to the virgin Mary and says, "Behold, you will conceive in your womb and bear a son, and you shall call his name Jesus." Mary is astounded and baffled. Virgins don't have sons. She could have scoffed and argued. But instead she said, "How will this be, since I am a virgin?" (Luke 1:34). She did not say it can't happen; she asked, "How?"

Contrast this with Gabriel's visit to Zechariah, the father of John the Baptist. The angel comes and tells him, "Your wife Elizabeth will bear you a son, and you shall call his name John" (Luke 1:13). But Zechariah knew that "Elizabeth was barren and advanced in years" (Luke 1:7). Different from Mary, his skepticism gave rise to a different question. He said, "How shall I know this?" Not: "How will you do this?" But: "How can I know you'll do it?"

Gabriel did not like this answer. He said, "I am Gabriel, who stands in the presence of God, and I was sent to speak to you and to bring you this good news. And behold, you will be silent and unable to speak until the day that these things take place, because you did not believe my words, which will be fulfilled in their time" (Luke 1:19–20).

So I conclude that humble, teachable questions about how and why God does what He does are acceptable to God. God gave a very helpful answer to Mary, "The Holy

Spirit will come upon you, and the power of the Most High will overshadow you" (Luke 1:35). This did not remove the mystery, but it helped.

I can't remove the mystery from Romans 9. But there is more to understand than we have seen, and I do not want to discourage you from pressing further up and further in to the heart and mind of God. Just do it with meekness and with willingness to affirm what He says, even if it is perplexing.

Don't let your prayers be an occasion for back-talking. Don't criticize or get angry at God. Soon enough we will be finished with this brief life of perplexity. "Now we see in a mirror dimly, but then face to face. Now I know in part; then I shall know fully, even as I have been fully known" (1 Corinthians 13:12). Be honest with God about your bewilderment. But put your hand on your mouth, if murmuring arises. Better to sit silently and wait for the explanation, than to say that one could not exist. "For God alone, O my soul, wait in silence, for my hope is from him" (Psalm 62:5).

Father, we confess that we are the children,
and You are the Father. We are the learners,
and You are the Teacher. We are sinful and fallible,
You are holy and all-wise.
Teach us to measure our thoughts
by Yours and not the other way around.
Humble us under Your mighty hand.
Forbid that we would get angry with You,
or criticize You, or be disappointed with You.
Make us tremble at such insults.
Oh, how deep are Your riches and Your wisdom!
How unsearchable Your judgments!
How inscrutable Your ways!
We praise You!
In Jesus' name,
Amen.

Twenty-Two

WHY I DO NOT SAY, "GOD DID NOT CAUSE THE CALAMITY, BUT HE CAN USE IT FOR GOOD."

Many Christians spoke this way about the murderous destruction of the World Trade Towers on September 11, 2001: "God did not cause it, but He can use it for good." Of course God can and does use our calamities for our good. I am not denying that. But that is very different from saying, "God did not cause the calamity." There are two reasons I do not say, "God uses, but does not cause calamity." One is that it goes beyond, and is contrary to, what the Bible teaches. The other is that it undermines the very hope it wants to offer.

First, this statement goes beyond and against the Bible. For some, all they want to say in denying that God "caused" the calamity is that God is not a sinner and that God does not remove human accountability and that God is compassionate. That is all true—and precious beyond words. But for others, and for most people who hear this slogan, something far more is implied. Namely, God, by His very nature, cannot or would not act to bring about such a calamity. This view of God is what contradicts the Bible and undercuts hope.

How God governs all events in the universe without sinning, and without removing responsibility from man, and with compassionate outcomes is mysterious indeed! But that is what the Bible teaches. God "works all things according to the counsel of his will" (Ephesians 1:11).

This "all things" includes the fall of sparrows (Matthew 10:29), the rolling of dice (Proverbs 16:33), the slaughter of His people (Psalm 44:11), the decisions of kings (Proverbs 21:1), the failing of sight (Exodus 4:11), the sickness of children (2 Samuel 12:15), the loss and gain of money (1 Samuel 2:7), the suffering of saints (1 Peter 4:19), the completion of travel plans (James 4:15), the persecution of Christians (Hebrews 12:4–7), the repentance of souls (2 Timothy 2:25), the gift of faith (Philippians 1:29), the pursuit of holiness (Philippians 3:12–13), the growth of believers (Hebrews 6:3), the giving and taking of life (1 Samuel 2:6), and the crucifixion of His Son (Acts 4:27–28).

From the smallest thing to the greatest thing, good and evil, happy and sad, pagan and Christian, pain and pleasure—God governs them all for His wise and just and good purposes (Isaiah 46:10). As the 27th question to the Heidelberg Catechism says,

> The almighty and everywhere present power of God; whereby, as it were by his hand, he upholds and governs heaven, earth, and all creatures; so that herbs and grass, rain and drought, fruitful and barren years, meat and drink, health and sickness, riches and poverty, yea, and all things come, not by chance, but be his fatherly hand.

Lest we miss the point, the Bible speaks most clearly to this in the most painful situations. Amos asks, in time of disaster, "Does disaster come to a city unless the LORD has done it?" (Amos 3:6). After losing all ten of his children in the collapse of his son's house, Job says, "The LORD gave, and the LORD has taken away; blessed be the name of the LORD" (Job 1:21). After being covered with boils he says, "Shall we receive good from God, and shall we not receive adversity?" (Job 2:10).

Oh, yes, Satan is real and active and involved in this world of woe! In fact Job 2:7 says, "Satan went out from the presence of the LORD and smote Job with sore boils from the sole of his foot to the crown of his head" (NASB).

Satan struck him. But Job did not get comfort from looking at secondary causes. He got comfort from looking at the ultimate cause. "Shall we not accept adversity from God?" And the author of the book agrees with Job when he says that Job's brothers and sisters "showed him sympathy and comforted him for all the evil that *the LORD* had brought upon him" (Job 42:11).

Then James underlines God's purposeful goodness in Job's misery: "You have heard of the steadfastness of Job, and you have seen the purpose of the Lord, how the Lord is compassionate and merciful" (James 5:11). Job himself concludes in prayer: "I know that you can do all things, and that no purpose of yours can be thwarted" (Job 42:2). Yes, Satan is real, and he is terrible—but he is on a leash.

The other reason I don't say, "God did not cause the calamity, but He can use it for good," is that it undercuts the very hope it wants to create. I ask those who say this: "If you deny that God could have 'used' a million prior events to save thousands of people from the World Trade Center collapse, what hope then do you have that God could now 'use' this terrible event to save you in the hour of trial?" Those who say God "can use the this calamity for good" nevertheless deny that He could "use" the events prior to 9-11 to prevent the evil itself. But the Bible teaches He could have restrained this evil (Genesis 20:6). "The LORD brings the counsel of the nations to nothing; he frustrates the plans of the peoples" (Psalm 33:10). Yet it was not in His plan to do it. Let us beware. We spare God the burden of His sovereignty and lose our only hope.

God is not like a firefighter who gets calls to show up at calamities when the damage is already happening. He is more like a surgeon who plans the cutting he must do and plans it for good purposes. Without the confidence that God rules over the beginning of our troubles, it is hard to believe that He could rule over their end. If we deny God His power and wisdom to govern the arrival of our pain, why should we think we can trust Him with its departure?

All of us are sinners. We deserve to perish. Every breath we take is an undeserved gift in this vapor-length life. We have one great hope: that Jesus Christ died to obtain pardon and righteousness for us (Ephesians 1:7; 2 Corinthians 5:21), and that God will employ His all-conquering, sovereign grace to preserve us for our inheritance (Jeremiah 32:40). We surrender this hope if we sacrifice this sovereignty.

Lord, have mercy on us
in our frail and fallible condition.
You are very powerful, and we are but grass.
We flourish and are gone.
Grant us grace to trust that You are good
in all Your works and all Your ways.
May we never doubt Your sovereignty,
even in the most painful times.
Let the bones which You have broken rejoice.
Though You cause grief, have compassion on us
according to Your steadfast love.
In Jesus' name,
Amen.

Twenty-Three

HOPE-GIVING PROMISES FOR TRIUMPH OVER SIN

One of the reasons sin will not rule as lord over us while we are "under grace" (Romans 6:14) is that, while we are under grace, God is at work in us to will and to do His good pleasure. I base this on Romans 6:17, which says, "But thanks be to God that though you were slaves of sin, you became obedient from the heart to that form of teaching to which you were committed" (NASB). Since Paul *thanks God* that the Romans became obedient from the heart, I conclude that God is the one who worked to bring about this obedience in their hearts. And if God works to bring about obedience in our heart, then sin won't be the lord over us—God will.

This does not mean we become perfect in this life (Philippians 3:12; 2 Corinthians 3:18; Romans 7:24), but it does mean that sin is dethroned in the castle of our lives and the defeat of sin is certain as we "fight the good fight of the faith" (1 Timothy 6:12) until we die or until Jesus comes (2 Timothy 4:7). I have heard the illustration that sanctification—our progressive war against sin and pursuit of holiness—is like a man spinning a yo-yo up and down as he goes up the stairs. Our lives have their ups and downs in the pursuit of godliness, but there is progress in rising overall toward the holiness we desire.

But I think the illustration needs one small correction. Halfway up the stairs we may have a temporary defeat in our warfare against unbelief and sin that sends the yo-yo of faith lower than it was on the first step. In other words, there is no guarantee in our battle with unbelief and sin, that the defeats of our later years will not bring discouragements and desperation worse than those of the early years. The battle must be fought to the very end, whether progression is steady or not.

We must let the sovereignty of God make us hopeful that change is possible, not passive as if no change were necessary. So take the following texts as encouragements from God that you can and you will make progress in driving sin from your life.

Second Thessalonians 1:11–12, "To this end we always pray for you, that our God may...fulfill every resolve for good and every work of faith by his power, so that the name of our Lord Jesus may be glorified in you." Remember, Christ gets the glory when it is manifest that God enables us to fulfill our good resolves through Him.

Hebrews 13:20–21, "Now may the God of peace…equip you with everything good that you may do his will, working in us that which is pleasing in his sight, through Jesus Christ, to whom be the glory forever and ever. Amen." Again, notice, since God enables us to do what is pleasing in His sight "through Jesus," it is Jesus who gets the glory, not us.

First Peter 4:11, "Whoever serves" is to do so *"as one who serves by the strength which God supplies—in order that in everything God may be glorified through Jesus Christ. To him belong glory and dominion forever and ever. Amen."* The giver gets the glory. Because God is the one who enables us to "serve" Him, He gets the credit for the service.

Galatians 5:22–23, "The fruit of the Spirit is love, joy, peace, patience, kindness, goodness, faithfulness, gentleness, self-control; against such things there is no law." Christian attitudes and behaviors are the fruit of the Spirit, not ultimately the fruit of our own efforts. Our efforts are essential, but not finally decisive. See below on Philippians 2:12–13.

All these texts I have mentioned are examples of how God fulfills the Old Testament promise of the New Covenant—the promise that God will work in His people to bring about obedience. Here are some examples of those Old Testament promises.

Jeremiah 31:31–33, "Behold, the days are coming,

declares the LORD, when I will make a new covenant with the house of Israel.... I will put my law within them, and I will write it on their hearts." Once, the Law was external on stone and met rebellion in our rebellious hearts. But in the New Covenant, however, God does not leave the Law outside, making demands; He also takes it inside, creating obedience.

Deuteronomy 30:6, "The LORD your God will circumcise your heart...so that you will love the LORD your God with all your heart and with all your soul."

Ezekiel 11:19–20, "A new spirit I will put within them. I will remove the heart of stone from their flesh and give them a heart of flesh, that they may walk in my statutes and keep my rules and obey them."

Ezekiel 36:26–27, "I will give you a new heart, and a new spirit I will put within you. And I will remove the heart of stone from your flesh and give you a heart of flesh. And I will put my Spirit within you, and cause you to walk in my statutes." Note the strong language of "cause you to walk in my statutes." That is what I think Paul was thanking God for in Romans 6:17.

Jeremiah 32:40, "I will make with them an everlasting covenant, that I will not turn away from doing good to them. I will put the fear of me in their hearts, that they may not turn from me." Our enduring to the end in the fear of God is owing to God's powerful grace to keep us.

How then should we pray and use our willpower? One

example from Paul for how to pray if God has promised to work His holy will into our lives: "May the Lord make you increase and abound in love for one another and for all" (1 Thessalonians 3:12; see Philippians 1:9–11). We ask God to do in us the very thing that He commands: "O Lord, make us abound in love to each other! This is your work! Do it!"

But praying does not replace working. God's sovereignty does not mean there is no such thing as human willpower. We are commanded to exert our wills in the cause of righteousness. "Work out your own salvation with fear and trembling, for it is God who works in you, both to will and to work for his good pleasure" (Philippians 2:12–13). It is the promise (God will work in you!) that sustains and gives hope to the willpower (work out your salvation). Take heart. God will not leave you to yourself.

Yes, Lord, we do take heart
from Your New Covenant promises.
They are the sweetest ones of all.
And from this side of the cross we see
that they are all blood bought and secure.
Thank You, Father, for sending Jesus Christ
to be for us, by His blood, the yes and the AMEN
to all Your promises. He is now the great ground
of our hope and joy. Don't let us despair
in the battle of this brief life.
In Jesus' name,
Amen.

Twenty-Four

JONATHAN EDWARDS ON THE PILGRIM MINDSET

The year 2003 was Jonathan Edwards' 300th birthday. It came as a timely reminder to me that this giant of the church, and one of my heroes, has much to teach the church today about treasuring Christ, and about the pilgrim mindset that marks the lives of those who treasure Christ above this world. In September, 1733, he preached a sermon called "The Christian Pilgrim, Or, The True Christian's Life a Journey Toward Heaven." It was based on Hebrews 11:13–14:

> These all died in faith, not having received the things promised, but having seen them and greeted them from afar, and having acknowledged that they were strangers and exiles on the earth.

For people who speak thus make it clear that they are seeking a homeland.

Let's listen in on Edwards' exposition, and let him shape our vision of what it means to live this vapor-length life as pilgrims on the way to heaven, treasuring Christ above all things.

Pilgrims are not diverted from their aim.

A traveler...is not enticed by fine appearances to put off the thought of proceeding. No, but his journey's end is in his mind. If he meets with comfortable accommodations at an inn, he entertains no thoughts of settling there. He considers that these things are not his own, that he is but a stranger, and when he has refreshed himself, or tarried for a night, he is for going forward. (*Works*, Banner of Truth, 243)

Pilgrims are to hold the things of this world loosely.

So should we desire heaven more than the comforts and enjoyments of this life.... Our hearts ought to be loose to these things, as that of a man on a journey, that we may as cheerfully part with them whenever God calls. (243)

Pilgrims become like what they hope to attain.

We should be endeavoring to come nearer to heaven, in being more heavenly, becoming more and more like the inhabitants of heaven in respect of holiness and conformity to God, the knowledge of God and Christ, in clear views of the glory of God, the beauty of Christ, and the excellency of divine things, as we come nearer to the beatific vision. We should labor to be continually growing in divine love—that this may be an increasing flame in our hearts, till they ascend wholly in this flame. (244)

Pilgrims will not be satisfied with anything less than God.

God is the highest good of the reasonable creature, and the enjoyment of him is the only happiness with which our souls can be satisfied. To go to heaven fully to enjoy God, is infinitely better than the most pleasant accommodations here. Fathers and mothers, husbands, wives, children, or the company of earthly friends, are but shadows. But the enjoyment of God is the substance. These are but scattered beams, but God is the sun. These are but streams, but God is the fountain. These are but drops, but God is the ocean....

Why should we labor for, or set our hearts on anything else, but that which is our proper end, and true happiness? (244)

Pilgrims are not grieved by their arrival at the journey's end.

To spend our lives so as to be only a journeying towards heaven, is the way to be free from bondage and to have the prospect and forethought of death comfortable. Does the traveler think of his journey's end with fear and terror? Is it terrible to him to think that he has almost got to his journey's end? Were the children of Israel sorry after forty years' travel in the wilderness, when they had almost got to Canaan? (246)

Pilgrims ponder what they pursue.

Labor to be much acquainted with heaven. If you are not acquainted with it, you will not be likely to spend your life as a journey thither. You will not be sensible of its worth, nor will you long for it. Unless you are much conversant in your mind with a better good, it will be exceeding difficult to you to have your hearts loose from these things, to use them only in subordination to something else, and be ready to part with them for the sake of that better good. Labor therefore to obtain a realizing sense of a heavenly world, to get a firm belief of its reality, and to be very much conversant with it in your thoughts. (246)

Pilgrims travel together.

Let Christians help one another in going this journey.... Company is very desirable in a journey, but in none so much as this. Let them go united and not fall out by the way, which would be to hinder one another, but use all means they can to help each other up the hill. This would ensure a more successful traveling and a more joyful meeting at their Father's house in glory. (246)

These are precious words from a man who finished his journey well. He was a pilgrim. And we may learn from him how to see this life as a vapor and see heaven as an everlasting joy. To live is Christ and to die is gain. Therefore let us learn to treasure Christ now above all things, and count everything as rubbish by comparison, so that our hearts will "be loose to these things, as that of a man on a journey, that we may as cheerfully part with them whenever God calls."

Amen, Lord! Grant that we
will love Christ above all things.
And may we spend our pilgrim life
learning to love this world less and heaven more.
Put us out of taste with the delicacies of the devil,
And give us a liking for the solid joys of Christ.
Guard us from the allurements of the lodgings
on this journey, and fix our eyes on the end.
And so, Father, make us useful to this world,
loving, helping, serving here,
while leading people up to God.
In Jesus' name,
Amen.

Twenty-Five

SOWN IN DISHONOR, RAISED IN GLORY

Romantic death is rare. More common are involuntary groanings and screams of pain. The ignominy of dying is pathetic. It is more often hellish than heroic. The apostle Paul uses two words to capture death's degrading assault. The first is "dishonor." He says that the death of our physical body is like a seed being sown in the ground. How is it sown? "It is sown in dishonor" (1 Corinthians 15:43).

During my college days, my father's mother died, leaving my grandfather very alone in Pennsylvania. His youngest son, my father, brought him to South Carolina to live with us. I was glad, and my mother was gracious, as always. Over time, his condition worsened and my mother was unable to care for him in the absence of my dad, who traveled as an evangelist.

So the painful decision was made to move him to a nursing home. There I watched him decline from the strong toolmaker-turned-pastor to skin-and-bones. The last time I saw him alive was with my father while I was home from seminary. We drove to the nursing home together, expressing the expectation that this would be the last time I would see him alive. It was.

There he lay in a diaper, curled up in a fetal position. His eyes were glazed over and crusty. His breathing was labored. My father spoke with me about his dad for a few minutes and then suggested we pray very loudly by putting our mouths next to his seemingly deaf ears. Ignoring the others in the home, we almost shouted our prayer. When my father stopped, his father heaved with all his fading might and said, "AMEN!" That was the last sound I ever heard him make. If I had ever seen a body sown in "dishonor," this was it. And there are millions like him.

Then there is another word that Paul uses to describe the humiliating condition of death. In Philippians 3:21 he says that Christ "shall change our vile body, that it may be fashioned like unto his glorious body" (KJV). The word "vile" translates the Greek, *tapeinōseōs*. Before the New Testament transformed this word into a virtue, because of Christ's glorious "lowliness," the word had only negative connotations of "humiliation, debasement, defeat."

I recall reading a biography of Julius Schniewind, a German New Testament scholar who was born in 1883. He became deathly ill in the summer of 1948, but few knew how serious it was. Hans-Joakim Kraus was with him when he taught his last "lay Bible hour," and heard him groan as he was leaving, "*Soma tapeinōseōs! Soma tapeinōseōs!*"—the phrase from Philippians 3:21: "Body of humiliation! Body of humiliation!"

Christianity is deeply aware of the humiliation, degradation, and dishonor of the body in death. The death of Jesus stamped forever our expectation. "His appearance was so marred, beyond human semblance, and his form beyond that of the children of mankind" (Isaiah 52:14). Is the disciple above his Lord? Should we expect anything better? His back was torn from scourging, His face swollen from punching, His head bloodied from the thorns and chin ripped because of the beard-pulling, His hands and feet swollen and mangled with the spikes, His side pierced with a large spear. And He was shamefully naked. He died with a "loud cry" (Mark 15:37).

How precious, therefore, to all followers of Jesus, that He rose from the dead with a "body of glory," never to die again! And how precious is the promise of Romans 6:5 that, "If we have become united with him in a death like his, we shall certainly be united with him in a resurrection like his." And the promise of 1 Corinthians 15:43, "It is sown in dishonor; *it is raised in glory.*" And the promise of

Philippians 3:21, "[He] will transform our lowly body to be like his glorious body." And the promise of Matthew 13:43, "Then the righteous will shine like the sun in the kingdom of their Father."

Merciful Father, help us be ready to die well.
Teach us how to help each other die!
You have shown us that it will not be easy.
But, oh, how many promises You have given
to help us say, "To die is gain."
Deliver us from fear.
Give us unshakeable hope.
Remind us that suffering may last
for the night, but joy comes in the morning.
Make us feel that this slight
momentary affliction, this vapor, is
working for us an eternal weight of glory.
In Jesus' name,
Amen.

Twenty-Six

THE FIERCE FRUIT OF
SELF-CONTROL

"As the Hebrews were promised the land, but had to take it by force, one town at a time, so we are promised the gift of self-control, yet we also must take it by force."[1]

The very concept of "self-control" implies a battle between a divided self. It implies that our "self" produces desires we should not gratify but instead "control." We should "deny ourselves," and "take up our cross daily," Jesus says, and follow Him (Luke 9:23). Daily our "self" produces desires that should be "denied" or "controlled."

The path that leads to heaven is narrow and strewn with suicidal temptations to abandon the way. Therefore

Jesus says, "Strive to enter through the narrow door" (Luke 13:24). The Greek word for "strive" is *agōnizesthe* in which you correctly hear the English word "agonize."

We get a taste of what is involved from Matthew 5:29, "If your right eye causes you to sin, tear it out and throw it away." This is the fierceness of self-control. This is what is behind the words of Jesus in Matthew 11:12, "The kingdom of heaven has suffered violence, and the violent take it by force." Are you laying hold on the kingdom fiercely?

Paul says that Christians exercise self-control like the Greek athletes, only our goal is eternal, not temporal. "Everyone who competes in the games (*agōnizomenos*) exercises self-control in all things. They then do it to receive a perishable wreath, but we an imperishable" (1 Corinthians 9:25, NASB). So he says, "I pommel my body and subdue it" (1 Corinthians 9:27, NASB). Self-control is saying no to sinful desires, even when it hurts.

But the Christian way of self-control is *not* "Just say no!" The problem is with the word "just." You don't *just* say no. You say no in a certain way: You say no by faith in the superior power and pleasure of Christ. The "No!" is just as ruthless. And maybe just as painful. But the difference between worldly self-control and godly self-control is crucial. Who will get the glory for victory? That's the issue. Will *we* get the glory? Or will *Christ* get the glory? If we exercise self-control by faith in Christ's superior power and pleasure, Christ will get the glory.

Fundamental to the Christian view of self-control is that it is a gift. It is the fruit of the Holy Spirit: "The fruit of the Spirit is love, joy, peace...self-control" (Galatians 5:22). How do we "strive" against our fatal desires? Paul answers: "I labor, striving (*agōnizomenos*) according to His power, which mightily works within me" (Colossians 1:29, NASB). The key is "according to His power." He "agonizes" by the power of Christ, not his own. Similarly he tells us, "If by the Spirit you put to death the deeds of the body, you will live" (Romans 8:13). "Not by might, nor by power, but by my Spirit, says the LORD of hosts" (Zechariah 4:6). We must be fierce! Yes. but not by *our* might. "The horse is made ready for the day of battle, but the victory belongs to the LORD" (Proverbs 21:31).

And how does the Spirit produce this fruit of self-control in us? By instructing us in the superior preciousness of grace, and enabling us to see and savor (that is, "trust") all that God is for us in Jesus. "The grace of God has appeared...training us to renounce...worldly passions...in the present age" (Titus 2:11–12). When we really see and believe what God is for us by grace through Jesus Christ, the power of wrong desires is broken. Therefore the fight for self-control is a fight of faith. "Fight the good fight of the faith. Take hold of the eternal life to which you were called" (1 Timothy 6:12).

1. Edward Welch, "Self-Control: The Battle Against 'One More,'" *The Journal of Biblical Counseling*, vol. 19, No. 2 (Winter, 2001): 30.

Father in heaven, we pray that You will work in us
the will to fight the suicidal sin that our will desires.
We confess that there is a war within us.
We grieve over the remnants of our corruption.
Help us to set our faces like flint
against the desire for anything above Christ.
And grant that we would treasure Him above all.
In His name, we pray,
Amen.

Twenty-Seven

THOUGHTS ON
GOD'S THOUGHTS

In a letter to George Bainton on October 15, 1888, Mark Twain said, "The difference between the almost right word and the right word is really a large matter—it's the difference between the lightning bug and the lightning."

So it is with the difference between the thought of a man and the thought of God. God's thoughts are our goal. We must be about finding, understanding, trusting, cherishing, obeying, and spreading the thoughts of God. Nothing matters more than what God has thought and spoken about everything, especially about Himself.

Our thoughts are ephemeral, but God's are eternal.

Psalm 94:11, "The LORD knows the thoughts of man, that they are but a breath."

Isaiah 40:7–8, "The grass withers, the flower fades when the breath of the LORD blows on it; surely the people are grass. The grass withers, the flower fades, but the word of our God will stand forever."

God's thoughts are countless.

Psalm 40:5, "You have multiplied, O LORD my God, your wondrous deeds and your thoughts toward us; none can compare with you! I will proclaim and tell of them, yet they are more than can be told."

Psalm 139:17, "How precious to me are your thoughts, O God! How vast is the sum of them!"

God's thoughts are immeasurably higher than our thoughts.

Isaiah 55:7–9, "Let the wicked forsake his way, and the unrighteous man his thoughts.... For my thoughts are not your thoughts, neither are your ways my ways, declares the LORD. For as the heavens are higher than the earth, so are my ways higher than your ways, and my thoughts than your thoughts."

God's thoughts are unsearchable and unfathomable.

Romans 11:33–36, "Oh, the depth of the riches and wisdom and knowledge of God! How unsearchable are his judgments and how inscrutable his ways! For who has known the mind of the Lord, or who has been his counselor? Or who has given a gift to him that he might be repaid? For from him and through him and to him are all things. To Him be glory forever. Amen."

God's thoughts can only be found out by God.

1 Corinthians 2:11, "For who knows a person's thoughts except the spirit of that person, which is in him? So also no one comprehends the thoughts of God except the Spirit of God."

God's thoughts are revealed to whom He pleases.

Matthew 11:25–27, "At that time Jesus declared, 'I thank you, Father, Lord of heaven and earth, that you have hidden these things from the wise and understanding and revealed them to little children; yes, Father, for such was your gracious will. All things have been handed over to me by my

Father; and no one knows the Son except the Father, and no one knows the Father except the Son and anyone to whom the Son chooses to reveal him.'"

God's thoughts are revealed through inspired spokesmen in the Bible.

First Corinthians 2:12–13, "Now we have received not the spirit of the world, but the Spirit who is from God, that we might understand the things freely given us by God. And we impart this in words not taught by human wisdom but taught by the Spirit, interpreting spiritual truths to those who are spiritual."

But the thoughts of God are ridiculed by the natural man.

First Corinthians 2:14, "The natural person does not accept the things of the Spirit of God, for they are folly to him, and he is not able to understand them because they are spiritually discerned."

We need a renewed mind to grasp the thoughts of God.

Romans 12:2, "Do not be conformed to this world, but be transformed by the renewal of your mind, that by testing you may discern what is the will of God, what is good and acceptable and perfect."

We are transformed to receive the thoughts of God by beholding God's glory.

Second Corinthians 3:18, "And we all, with unveiled face, beholding the glory of the Lord, are being transformed into the same image from one degree of glory to another. For this comes from the Lord who is the Spirit."

We behold the glory of God by a miracle of God's creative act through the gospel.

Second Corinthians 4:4–6, "In their case the god of this world has blinded the minds of the unbelievers, to keep them from seeing the light of the gospel of the glory of Christ, who is the image of God. For what we proclaim is not ourselves, but Christ Jesus as Lord, with ourselves as your servants for Jesus' sake. For God, who said, 'Let light shine out of darkness,' has shone in our hearts to give the light of the knowledge of the glory of God in the face of Jesus Christ."

Thus renewed, we pursue the thoughts of God like silver and gold.

Proverbs 2:1–6, "My son, if you receive my words and treasure up my commandments within you, making your ear attentive to wisdom and inclining your heart to understanding; yes, if you call out for insight and raise your voice for understanding, if you seek it like silver and search for it as for hidden treasures, then you will understand the fear of the LORD and find the knowledge of God. For the LORD gives wisdom; from his mouth come knowledge and understanding."

The Lord gives understanding of His thoughts through serious thinking about them.

Second Timothy 2:7, "Think over what I say, for the Lord will give you understanding in everything."

Knowledge of God's thoughts puffs up, but love builds up.

First Corinthians 8:1–3, "Now concerning food offered to idols: we know that 'all of us possess knowledge.' This 'knowledge' puffs up, but love builds up. If anyone imagines that he knows something, he does not yet know as he ought to know. But if anyone loves God, he is known by God."

All knowledge of God's thoughts is for the sake of love.

First Timothy 1:5, "The aim of our charge is love that issues from a pure heart and a good conscience and a sincere faith."

But all love is for the sake of the glory of and praise of God.

Philippians 1:9–11, "It is my prayer that your love may abound more and more, with knowledge and all discernment, so that you may approve what is excellent, and so be pure and blameless for the day of Christ, filled with the fruit of righteousness that comes through Jesus Christ, to the glory and praise of God."

Now this is remarkable—all of God's thoughts aiming to help us love each other; and all of our love aiming at "the praise and glory of God." This double truth is one of God's great thoughts. God has acted and spoken so that we might love each other and in loving each other show God to be glorious.

But how can this be? How does this great thought of God work? Isn't love an end in itself? How can you really love someone and have an ulterior motive—that God be glorified? The answer is one of God's thoughts toward us that is precious beyond words. It goes like this: Love is doing what will enthrall the beloved with the greatest and longest joy. What will enthrall the beloved this way is the glory of God. Love *means* doing all we can, at whatever cost to ourselves, to help people be enthralled with the glory of God. When they are, they are satisfied and God is glorified. Therefore loving people and glorifying God are one.

This is only one of the many discoveries we will make as we spend our days thinking the thoughts of God after Him. Seeing a thought of God for what it really is, and seeing a thought of a mere man is the difference between seeing lightning and a lightning bug.

So, Father, open our minds, enlarge our minds,
fill our minds, transform our minds,
so that we think Your thoughts after You.
Incline our hearts to Your word,
and not to getting gain.
Have mercy on us in our
foolish addictions to things
that dull us to the delights
of knowing You in Your Word.
You have multiplied, O LORD our God,
Your wondrous thoughts toward us.
Your thoughts are very deep!
All praise and honor to You!
In Jesus' name,
Amen.

Twenty-Eight

IS GOD'S DEMAND
FOR WORSHIP VAIN?

An Open Letter to Michael Prowse

Dear Mr. Prowse,

It would be my great joy to persuade you that God's demand for worship is beautiful love, not ugly pride. On March 30, 2003 you wrote in the *London Financial Times:*

> Worship is an aspect of religion that I always found difficult to understand. Suppose we postulate an omnipotent being who, for reasons inscrutable to us, decided to create something other than Himself. Why should he...expect us to worship him? We didn't ask to be created. Our lives are often troubled. We know that human tyrants, puffed up with pride, crave adulation and homage. But a morally perfect God would surely have no character defects. So why are all those

people on their knees every Sunday?

I don't understand why you assume that the only incentive for God to demand praise is that He is needy and defective. This is true for mere humans. But with God there is another possibility.

What if, as the atheist Ayn Rand once said, admiration is the rarest and best of pleasures? And what if, as I wish Ayn Rand could have seen, God really is the most admirable being in the universe? Would this not imply that God's summons for our praise is the summons for our highest joy? And if the success of that summons cost Him the life of His Son, would that not be love (instead of arrogance)?

The reason the Bible gives why God should be greatly praised is that He *is* great. "Great is the LORD, and greatly to be praised" (Psalm 96:4). He is more admirable than anything He has made. That is what it means to be God.

Moreover, the Bible says that praise—overflowing, heartfelt admiration—is a pleasure. "Praise the LORD! For it is good to sing praises to our God; for it is pleasant" (Psalm 147:1). And this pleasure is the best there is and lasts forever. "In [God's] presence there is fullness of joy; at your right hand are pleasures forevermore" (Psalm 16:11).

The upshot of this is that God's demand for supreme praise is His demand for our supreme happiness. Deep in our hearts we know that we were not made to be made much of. We were made to make much of something great. The best joys are when we forget ourselves, enthralled with greatness. The greatest greatness is God's. Every good that ever thrilled the heart of man is amplified ten thousand times in God, its Maker. God is in a class by Himself. He is the only being for whom self-exaltation is essential to love. If He "humbly" sent us away from His beauty, suggesting we find our joy in another, we would be ruined.

Great thinkers have said this long before I did. For example, Jonathan Edwards said:

> It is easy to conceive how God should seek the good of the creature...even his happiness, from a supreme regard to himself; as his happiness arises from...the creature's exercising a supreme regard to God...in loving it, and rejoicing in it.... God's respect to the creature's good, and his respect to himself, is not a divided respect; but both are united in one, as the happiness of the creature aimed at is happiness in union with himself. (Jonathan Edwards, *The End for Which God Created the World*, in John Piper, *God's Passion for His Glory* [Wheaton, Ill.: Crossway Books, 1998], 248f.)

C. S. Lewis broke through to the beauty of God's self-exaltation (thinking at first, like you, that the Psalms sounded like an old woman craving compliments). He finally saw the obvious:

> My whole, more general, difficulty about the praise of God depended on my absurdly denying to us, as regards the supremely Valuable, what we delight to do, what indeed we can't help doing, about everything else we value. I think we delight to praise what we enjoy because the praise not merely expresses but completes the enjoyment; it is its appointed consummation. (C. S. Lewis, *Reflections on the Psalms* [New York: Harcourt, Brace and World, 1958], 93–5)

Both Edwards and Lewis saw that praising God is the consummation of joy in God. This joy flows from the infinite beauty and greatness of God. There is no one who surpasses Him in any truly admirable trait. He is absolutely enjoyable. But we are sinners and do not see it, and do not want it. We want ourselves at the center. But Jesus Christ taught us to be human in another way, and then died for our sin, absorbed God's wrath against us, and opened the way to see and savor God. "Christ suffered once for sins, the righteous for the unrighteous, that he might bring us to God" (1 Peter 3:18).

Therefore, the reason God seeks our praise is not because He won't be complete until He gets it. He is seeking our praise because we won't be complete until we give it. This is not arrogance. It is love.

I pray that you will see and savor the beauty of your Maker and your Redeemer.

John Piper

Father, indeed we do pray for Michael Prowse,
but not for him only, but for ourselves also.
We have not seen and savored You as we ought.
We have not worshiped You
with the white-hot affections that You deserve.
We have been lukewarm and half-hearted.
Forgive us, O Lord, our merciful God.
And lead us now into lasting joy.
Enthrall us with Yourself.
And break the power
of all lesser pleasures.
In Jesus' name,
Amen.

Twenty-Nine

TAKING THE SWAGGER
OUT OF CHRISTIAN
CULTURAL INFLUENCE

The fact that Christians are exiles on the earth (1 Peter 2:11), does not mean that they don't care what becomes of culture. But it does mean that they exert their influence as very happy, brokenhearted outsiders. We are exiles. "Our citizenship is in heaven, and from it we await a Savior, the Lord Jesus Christ" (Philippians 3:20). "Here we have no lasting city, but we seek the city that is to come" (Hebrews 13:14). Life is a vapor, lived in a foreign land.

But we are very happy sojourners, because we have been commanded by our bloody Champion to rejoice in exile miseries. "Blessed are you when others...persecute you...on my account. Rejoice and be glad, for your reward is great in heaven" (Matthew 5:11–12). We are happy because the apostle Paul showed us that "the sufferings of this present time are not worth comparing with the glory that is to be revealed to us" (Romans 8:18). We are happy because there are merciful foretastes everywhere in this fallen world, and God is glad for us to enjoy them (1 Timothy 4:3; 6:17). And we are happy because we know that the exiles will one day inherit the earth (Matthew 5:5). Christ died for sinners so that "all things" might one day belong to His people (Romans 8:32).

But our joy is a *brokenhearted* joy. Christ is worthy of so much better obedience than we Christians render. Our joy is a brokenhearted joy because so many people around the world have not heard the good news that "Christ Jesus came into the world to save sinners" (1 Timothy 1:15). And our joy is a brokenhearted joy because human culture—in every society—dishonors Christ, glories in its shame, and is bent on self-destruction.

This includes America. American culture does not belong to Christians, neither in reality nor in biblical theology. It never has. The present tailspin toward Sodom is not a fall from Christian ownership. "The whole world lies in the power of the evil one" (1 John 5:19). It has since the fall, and it will till Christ comes in open triumph. God's rightful ownership will be manifest in due time. The Lordship of Christ over all Creation is being manifest in stages, first the age of groaning, then the age of glory. "We ourselves, who have the firstfruits of the Spirit, groan inwardly as we wait eagerly for adoption as sons, the redemption of our bodies" (Romans 8:23). The exiles are groaning with the whole Creation. We are waiting.

But Christian exiles are not passive. We do not smirk at the misery or the merrymaking of immoral culture. We weep. Or we should. This is my main point: Being exiles does not mean being cynical. It does not mean being indifferent or uninvolved. The salt of the earth does not mock rotting meat. Where it can, it saves and seasons. And where it can't, it weeps. And the light of the world does not withdraw, saying "good riddance" to godless darkness. It labors to illuminate. But not dominate.

Being Christian exiles in American culture does not end our influence; it takes the swagger out of it. We don't get cranky that our country has been taken away. We don't whine about the triumphs of evil. We are not hardened with anger. We understand. This is not new. This was the way it was in the beginning—Antioch, Corinth, Athens, Rome. The Empire was not just degenerate, it was deadly. For three explosive centuries Christians paid for their Christ-exalting joy with blood. Many still do. More will.

It never occurred to those early exiles that they should rant about the ubiquity of secular humanism. The Imperial words were still ringing in their ears: "You will be hated by all for my name's sake. But the one who endures to the end will be saved" (Mark 13:13). This was a time for indomitable joy and unwavering ministries of mercy.

Yes, it was a time for influence—as it is now. But not with huffing and puffing as if to reclaim our lost laws. Rather with tears and persuasion and perseverance, knowing that the folly of racism, and the exploitation of the poor, and the de-God-ing of education, and the horror of abortion, and the collapse of heterosexual marriage are the tragic death-tremors of joy, not the victory of the left or the right.

The greatness of Christian exiles is not success but service. Whether we win or lose, we witness to the way of truth and beauty and joy. We don't own culture, and we don't rule it. We serve it with brokenhearted joy and long-suffering mercy, for the good of man and the glory of Jesus Christ.

＊

And so, Father, take the swagger
out of our indignation.
Take self-pity out of our hearts,
and presumption from our lips.
Make us feel that mercy is our life.
Teach us deeply that freely we have received,
and freely we must give.
Make us brokenhearted,
happy, useful sojourners.
In Jesus' name, we pray,
Amen.

Thirty

THE SWEET COMMANDS OF GOD TO DEMONS, WIND, RAVENS, AND LOVE

If, by God's grace, you are assured that God is for you and not against you, then the more evidences you find of God's sovereignty, the happier you are. And the wider the scope of God's sovereignty, the more secure you feel in all the perils of love.

And He *is* for us. The gospel is the good news that, because of Christ's blood and righteousness, we are justified by faith alone, and God is for us forever. In Romans 8:31–33 Paul says, "If God is for us, who can be against us?... Who shall bring any charge against God's elect?"

So, if God is for us, then all His power is on our side. All His sovereignty is exerted for our good and never against us. All His decrees are for our ultimate benefit. How sovereign is God over the things that threaten our lives? When God commands, who and what must obey?

Let's start at the highest enemy level. Good angels and evil spirits must obey God when He commands them with omnipotent authority: "Bless the Lord, O you his angels, you mighty ones who do his word, obeying the voice of his word!" (Psalm 103:20). "He commands even the unclean spirits, and they obey him" (Mark 1:27). So no demon can do anything to God's elect except serve the ultimate purposes of God who is for us. For example, consider 2 Corinthians 12:7–9,

> To keep me from being too elated by the surpassing greatness of the revelations, a thorn was given me in the flesh, a messenger of Satan to harass me, to keep me from being too elated. 8 Three times I pleaded with the Lord about this, that it should leave me. 9 But he said to me, "My grace is sufficient for you, for my power is made perfect in weakness." Therefore I will boast all the more gladly of my weaknesses, so that the power of Christ may rest upon me.

Paul's thorn in the flesh is "a messenger of Satan." Satan's design is Paul's misery and the ruin of his faith. He wants Paul to curse God, the way he wanted Job to curse God. Paul prayed that this "messenger of Satan" be removed. The risen Christ said no three times. Then he gave his reason: His own divine power would be magnified in Paul's weakness. In other words, Christ's design for this thorn and Satan's design are exactly the opposite. Satan wants to ruin Paul's faith and dishonor Christ. Christ wants it to refine Paul's faith and honor His power. The irony here is that Satan's torment backfires and becomes a means of sanctification—it must gall him when God does this. God knew he would do this when he permitted Satan to afflict Paul. Therefore, even Satan is part of God's design to bless Paul with greater usefulness and glorify the power of Christ.

Then let's consider the apparent enemy of the natural world that often hurts us with calamity and disaster and disease and obstruction. How sovereign is God over nature? What parts of nature can He command with effective power? Here are some biblical examples:

"I have commanded the ravens to feed you there" (1 Kings 17:4). "Have you commanded the morning since your days began, and caused the dawn to know its place?" (Job 38:12). "He commanded the skies above...and he rained down on them manna" (Psalm 78:23–24). "[He] commands the sun, and it does not rise; [He] seals up the stars" (Job 9:7). "The LORD appointed a great fish to swallow up Jonah" (Jonah 1:17). "The LORD God appointed a plant and made it come up over Jonah" (Jonah 4:6). "God appointed a worm that attacked the plant, so that it withered" (Jonah 4:7). "He commanded and raised the stormy wind, which lifted up the waves of the sea" (Psalm 107:25). "Who then is this, that he commands even winds and water, and they obey him?" (Luke 8:25). "He sends out his command to the earth; his word runs swiftly. He gives snow like wool; he scatters hoarfrost like ashes" (Psalm 147:15). "He hurls down his crystals of ice like crumbs; who can stand before his cold?" (Psalm 147:17). "I will also command the clouds that they rain no rain upon it" (Isaiah 5:6). "He covers his hands with the lightning and commands it to strike the mark" (Job 36:32).

If God commands all demons and all natural elements, and they obey Him, and if God is always for us and not against us, then everything that befalls the elect is for our good. Everything. "All things work together for good for those who love him and are called according to his purpose" (Romans 8:28) because He rules all things and is only for us and not against us.

Is that not the point of Jesus' logic when He said, "Are not two sparrows sold for a penny? And not one of them will fall to the ground apart from your Father.... Fear not, therefore; you are of more value than many sparrows" (Matthew 10:29, 31)? The logic here is that fear would be warranted if God did not rule tiny events like sparrow-deaths. But since He does rule over them, and since you are more valuable than sparrows, fear is *not* warranted. It's the sovereignty of God (no bird dies without Him) and the mercy of God (He cherishes you more) that takes away fear when it feels like the world is out of control.

But the sweetest commands of God are not commands to demons and ravens and wind. They are the commands to His own love and blessing and covenant. "By day the LORD commands his steadfast love, and at night his song is with me" (Psalm 42:8). "For there the LORD has commanded the blessing, life forevermore" (Psalm 133:3). "He sent redemption to his people; he has commanded his covenant forever. Holy and awesome is his name!" (Psalm 111:9). The sweetest commands God gives to his own love: Love, go out to my people with omnipotent power!

Awesome indeed!

Lord, let us never cease to marvel
at Your mercy and Your might!
These are the twin wonders along with Your wisdom
that give us hope when all around our soul gives way.
Your mercy, Your might, Your wisdom!
You are very great, and we praise You.
Strengthen us the way You did Paul
by word and, if necessary, by affliction.
May Satan's devices in our lives
ever be turned against his evil designs
and made to serve Your righteous ones.
Grant us always to believe that
Your invisible hand rules the world
and is ruled by a heart of holy love
and perfect wisdom.
In Jesus' name,
Amen.

Thirty-One

CHRIST SUFFERED AND DIED TO DELIVER US FROM THE PRESENT EVIL AGE

Meditation on Galatians 1:4

[He] gave himself for our sins to deliver us from the present evil age, according to the will of our God and Father.

Until we die, or until Christ returns to establish His kingdom, we live in "the present evil age." Therefore, when the Bible says that Christ gave Himself "to deliver us from the present evil age," it does not mean that He will take us out of the world, but that He will deliver us from the power of the evil in it. Jesus prayed for us like this: "I do not ask that you take them out of the world, but that you keep them from the evil one" (John 17:15).

The reason Jesus prays for deliverance from "the evil one" is that "this present evil age" is the age when Satan is given freedom to deceive and destroy. The Bible says, "The whole world lies in the power of the evil one" (1 John 5:19). This "evil one" is called "the god of this world," and his main tactic is blinding people to truth. "The god of this world has blinded the minds of the unbelievers, to keep them from seeing the light of the gospel of the glory of Christ" (2 Corinthians 4:4).

Until we waken to our darkened spiritual condition, we live in sync with "the present evil age" and the ruler of it. "You once walked, following the course of this world, following the prince of the power of the air, the spirit that is now at work in the sons of disobedience" (Ephesians 2:2). Without knowing it, we were lackeys of the devil. What felt like freedom was bondage. The Bible speaks straight to 21st century fads, fun, and addictions when it says, "They promise them freedom, but they themselves are slaves of corruption. For whatever overcomes a person, to that he is enslaved" (2 Peter 2:19).

The resounding cry of freedom in the Bible is: "Do not be conformed to this world, but be transformed by the renewal of your mind" (Romans 12:2). In other words, be free! Don't be duped by the gurus of the age. They are here today and gone tomorrow. One enslaving fad follows another. Thirty years from now today's tattoos will not be marks of freedom, but indelible reminders of conformity.

The wisdom of this age is folly in view of eternity. "Let no one deceive himself. If anyone among you thinks that he is wise in this age, let him become a fool that he may become wise. For the wisdom of this world is folly with God.... The word of the cross is folly to those who are perishing" (1 Corinthians 3:18–19; 1:18). What then is the wisdom of God in this age? It is the great liberating death of Jesus Christ. The early followers of Jesus said, "We preach Christ crucified...the power of God and the *wisdom of God*" (1 Corinthians 1:23–24).

When Christ went to the cross, He set millions of captives free. He unmasked the devil's fraud and broke his power. That's what He meant on the eve of His crucifixion when He said, "Now will the ruler of this world be cast out" (John 12:31). Don't follow a defeated foe. Follow Christ. It is costly. You will be an exile in this age. But you will be free.

And it will all be very soon. "With the Lord one day is as a thousand years, and a thousand years as one day" (2 Peter 3:8). Life is a vapor. Even two thousand years of lives are a vapor with God. "As for man, his days are like grass; he flourishes like a flower of the field; for the wind passes over it, and it is gone, and its place knows it no more" (Psalm 103:15–16). Only one life, 'twill soon be past, only what's done for Christ will last. What a tragedy when we fail to see that Christ, by His death and resurrection, has freed us from this evil age—from everything that we would look back on and say: wasted.

Therefore, attach yourself to the gospel of Christ. This alone will turn your earthly vapor into everlasting life. "For 'all flesh is like grass and all its glory like the flower of grass. The grass withers, and the flower falls, but the word of the Lord remains forever.' And this word is the good news that was preached to you" (1 Peter 1:24–25).

Come quickly, Lord Jesus!
And while You tarry, keep us free
from the sin of this world.
Oh, make our little lives count
for the glory of Your name
and for the fame of Your Father.
Rivet our attention on Your cross,
and fuse our affections to Yourself.
Waken our compassion for all who suffer,
especially those who are rushing toward
everlasting misery because of unbelief.
So open our mouths and open our hands
and open our wallets while we have breath,
and make us the most radically loving people
on earth, for the joy of all peoples
and the renown of Your name,
Amen.

❈ desiringGod

Desiring God exists to spread a passion for the supremacy of God in all things for the joy of all peoples through Jesus Christ. John Piper receives no royalties personally from the books he writes—they are all reinvested back into the ministry of Desiring God. It's all designed as part of our vision to spread this passion to others.

With that in mind, we invite you to visit the Desiring God website at desiringGod.org. You'll find twenty years' worth of free sermons by John Piper—in manuscript and downloadable audio formats—hundreds of free articles, and information about our upcoming conferences. An online store allows you to purchase audio albums, God-centered children's curriculum, books and resources by Noël Piper, and over 25 books by John Piper. You can also find information about our growing radio ministry at desiringGodradio.org.

DG also has a whatever-you-can-afford policy, designed for individuals without discretionary funds. If you'd like more information about this policy, please contact us at the address or phone number below.

We exist to help you make God your treasure. If we can serve you in any way, please let us know!

Desiring God
2601 East Franklin Avenue
Minneapolis, MN 55406-1103

Telephone: 1.888.346.4700
Fax: 612.338.4372
Email: mail@desiringGod.org
Web: www.desiringGod.org

Desiring God Europe
Unit 9-10 Spencer House
14-22 Spencer Road
Londonderry
Northern Ireland
BT47 6AA

Telephone/Fax: 011.44.28.713.429.07
Email: info@christisall.com
Web: www.christisall.com/dgm

Listen and Tremble...

"The voice of the LORD twists the oaks and strips the forest bare."
—Psalm 29:9

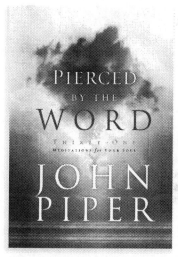

1-59052-173-0

Whether you're steeped in the Word of God or newly acquainted with it, these thirty-one meditations will penetrate to the deepest reaches of your soul.

With a contagious passion, John Piper awakens us to violent prayer, piercing pleasure, and fearless faith.

> *"May these meditations become in your life the living embodiment of God's Word and penetrate to the deep places of your soul. God has a good work to do there."*

DON'T MISS THESE TITLES from JOHN PIPER

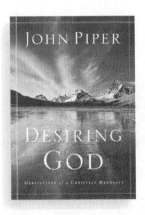
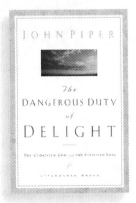

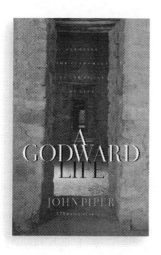

A Godward Life

Make God the center of your life and discover the radical difference by reading these 120 passionate thought-provoking devotions.

ISBN 1-57673-839-6

A Godward Life: Book Two

This follow-up to the popular *A Godward Life* is made up of 120 daily meditations that are solid meat and sweet milk from God's Word. They will brace your mind with truth and nourish your heart with God's sovereign grace.

ISBN 1-57673-405-6

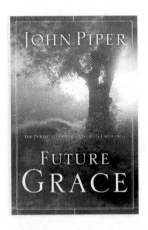

Future Grace

This book shows how the power of superior promises will sever the root of deceptive sin. It exposes the lie of Judas-joys.

ISBN 1-57673-337-8

The Pleasures of God

"God is most glorified in us when we are most satisfied in Him." This new edition of a classic by John Piper will further explore a life-changing essential—and again put God at the center, leaving the reader satisfied in Him.

ISBN 1-57673-665-2

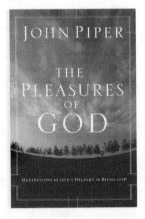

Printed in the United States
by Baker & Taylor Publisher Services